Living Well with Cancer

To Linda & Chris –

In appreciation of your

ministry over many

years

Damian

Living Well with Cancer:

A Solution-Focused Approach

By

Dominic Bray

**Cambridge
Scholars**
Publishing

Living Well with Cancer: A Solution-Focused Approach

By Dominic Bray

This book first published 2022. The present binding first published 2022.

Cambridge Scholars Publishing

Lady Stephenson Library, Newcastle upon Tyne, NE6 2PA, UK

British Library Cataloguing in Publication Data
A catalogue record for this book is available from the British Library

ISBN (10): 1-5275-8721-5
ISBN (13): 978-1-5275-8721-2

TABLE OF CONTENTS

The Book in a Page vii

Acknowledgements viii

Preface ix

Chapter One 1
The importance of a *good listening to*

Chapter Two 17
You are not alone; experiences of 'being in the same boat'

Start reading here if you like to 'cut to the chase'

Chapter Three 29
Cancer. The end… or a new beginning?

Chapter Four 53
Recruiting what you already know

Chapter Five 70
Next steps in this alternative life: "How do you eat an elephant?"

*Only keep reading if you're interested in the 'under the bonnet'
aspects of a solution-focused appointment and what else is out there.*

Chapter Six 92
The 'solution-focused' approach: more on what it is (and what it
isn't)

Chapter Seven.. 113
From the horse's mouth – a doctor's second opinion

Chapter Eight... 128
From the horse's mouth – confessions of a pharmacist

Chapter Nine.. 139
From the horse's mouth – a *second* doctor's opinion

Chapter Ten 153
The usual end bits

Bibliography/Resources 155

About the Author.. 161

THE BOOK IN A PAGE

'Courage is being scared to death... but saddling up anyway'[1]

This book is about that 'both/and' approach to, what may be for you, the hardest challenge you've ever had to face. It follows the pattern of many appointments I've been involved in over the years. Starting with a recognition of the lived experience of diagnosis and treatment, a crucial part of 'being heard', it then moves on to discuss how, by using *solution-focused* thinking, life may be lived well, whether it's for a very short, or ultimately a very long, time.

Written in an informal style, as if the reader is taking part in a chatty-but-powerfully-effective appointment, it is for people of any age who have, or have previously had, cancer and their families and friends... and includes some bonus 'clever bits' for health professionals who seek to help them. It is also highly relevant to other profoundly life-changing conditions.

It may be especially useful if, for whatever reason, you don't have access to someone who can offer this sort of appointment. It's mercifully short (not only because it's all I have to say), *but also* because you have a life to get on with; reading books like this may not be, and maybe *should* not be, your top priority. The *aim* is to validate and inspire. And, just possibly, entertain...

---

[1] John Wayne (1907-1979)

ACKNOWLEDGEMENTS

I'd like to thank everybody whom I've ever met.

But most of all my accountant.

PREFACE

It's quite common to see books that have a long-winded, often tedious preface you feel you'd better read in case you miss something. This isn't one of them.

By the way, all views expressed in this manuscript are that of the author and do not reflect those of any other entity, including, but not limited to, the Publisher, the NHS and any other affiliated charities.

CHAPTER ONE

THE IMPORTANCE OF A *GOOD LISTENING TO*

***The single biggest problem in communication is the illusion
that it has taken place[2]***

Once upon a time, perhaps some time that feels long ago, you were
getting on with your life.

In that life you were busy, meeting obligations, chasing lists of tasks,
doing what needed to be done to make a home and/or earn money
somewhere. Some things bothered you and you complained about the
weather, the kids not getting ready for school, other people's kids,
the price of petrol, call centres, bad driving…

---

[2] George Bernard Shaw (1856 – 1950)

[3] I've included these summaries at the beginning of chapters for my
colleagues with short concentration spans… like medics. Only joking… By
the way, this is a good opportunity to insert a disclaimer to the effect that
the views I express are my own and do not necessarily reflect those of my
employer (the NHS), any particular charity or anyone else who knows me
or who might not want to afterwards.

Ah... if only...

The past was a great place, as it turns out. Because the present is, frankly, a bit ****[4]

'What?' I hear the reader gasp. 'Shouldn't this weighty tome be all about solutions, living well, positive thinking and all that?' Well, yes, it is. With the possible exception of the last—there's a section later called 'Positive Thinking Makes Me Sick'.

However, the lived reality I've heard, sitting in small rooms with disappointed people[56], is that these worthy aims are not where the conversation starts.

Are you sitting comfortably?

...then let's begin. Chances are if you're reading this, you've either had a cancer diagnosis yourself and are interested in exploring 'what better might yet look like' in your life ... or you know a family member/friend/patient[7] who has/had cancer themselves and you want to help them. If it's the latter, please bear with me as I address my comments for now to the patient...

---

[4] Insert your favourite expletive here

[5] I've stuck in lots of footnotes so as not to break up the flow of the story, and for people who like me generally don't read them because they want to get on with it.

[6] One definition of a psychologist is *someone who sits down in a small room with disappointed people and tries to talk them out of it.* It's not original to me; I heard it at a conference so can't attribute it. Similarly, 'what's the difference between a psychologist and a psychiatrist? About fifty grand and a prescription pad'.

[7] I use the word 'patient' here as that's what's standard in hospitals and that designation seems to be generally acceptable to...er...patients. Other psychologists refer to 'clients' or 'service users'. However, people on the end of helping services themselves don't necessarily like these terms, which, as ever, shows 'you can't please everybody'! Now, if as a patient/client/service user you are disrespected, that IS a different story...

So how does the world, and, more to the point, life, look to you?

Most likely, *different.*

So, as you're gathering, I firmly believe that what people really need is a good listening to[8]. And, truth be told, this doesn't always happen in healthcare. This is often part of people's back-stories, often the first thing I hear in an appointment. So, I'm going to start with common experiences I've heard and the reasons, some excusable, some not, why they happen.

A question of the availability of time

Frequently, health services[9] are stretched. As medical technology gets ever better at keeping people alive into old age, so professionals become ever busier, helping ever more people[10]. Well done, by the way, to my medical colleagues (and researchers etc.) for achieving that! Seriously.

But, and here's the rub, the perception amongst many of my colleagues is 'I wish I could do more listening, but I just don't have the time'. My come-back is 'you don't have the time *not* to listen', but that's another argument[11]. The point here is that many patients have not had sufficient time afforded to them, especially by people traditionally seen as being of high status like medical consultants. Patients have not had a chance to tell their story, which causes added anxiety as consultants are often the decision-makers, the very ones to whom they, the patients, need to get through. Ironically, it's the

---

[8] Mary Lou Casey
[9] I'm writing this from the perspective of the British NHS but many of the same challenges apply elsewhere.
[10] More elegantly, 'delivering interventions'
[11] For an excellent book written by a medical doctor who's just about done it all, see Youngson, R (2012) *Time to Care*. Raglan (NZ): Rebelheart. He argues that investing time in listening can actually *save* time.

very same thing, anxiety (in this case, concerning caseloads and opening cans of worms), that is hamstringing these professionals[12].

A question of 'fixing'

Sometimes patients have the experience of remedies being offered to them that either don't fit or are premature, given before they've had a chance to be 'heard'. A bit like this[13]:

Patient : I feel like my world's falling apart.
Doctor : I can give you some antibiotics.

This may be due to a perceived pressure of time on the part of the health professional who wants to 'cut to the chase', or may be because the health professional quite likes being the one with the

---

[12] See an excellent paper: https://www.health.org.uk/publications/when-doctors-and-patients-talk-making-sense-of-the-consultation (Health Foundation, 2012, accessed 10/06/2022).

[13] The monochrome cartoons in this book are by Suparna B, who can be contacted via illuminecreations01@gmail.com

answers[14] (or feels a pressure to be, or indeed struggles with a 'non-fixing model[15]). This poem[16] illustrates the scenario nicely:

PLEASE LISTEN
When I ask you to listen to me
and you start to give me advice,
you have not done what I asked.
When I ask you to listen to me
and you begin to tell me why
I shouldn't feel that way,
you are trampling on my feelings.
When I ask you to listen to me
and you feel you have to do something to solve my problems,
you have failed me, strange as that may seem.
When you do something for me
that I can and need to do for myself,
you contribute to my fear and weakness.
So, please listen and just hear me, and
if you want to talk, wait a minute,
for your turn; and I will listen to you…

A question of unfair treatment

It may also be that the 'practical' things haven't gone well. Was there a delay in diagnosis with missed opportunities? Did someone fail to listen to crucial clinical information that could have made all the

---

[14] For a fuller discussion on this and what might help health professionals to change their approach, see Bray, D. et al. (2020) *Unleashing the Solution-Focused Power of the Ormskirk Model by Minding Your Language* Diabetes Care for Children & Young People 10 (1) p.58.
(https://diabetesonthenet.com/diabetes-care-children-young-people/ unleashing-the-solution-focused-power-of-the-ormskirk-model-by-minding-your-language/)
[15] For example, Fox, E. (1997) Predominance of the Curative Model of Medical Care: A Residual Problem. JAMA. 278(9) 761-763.
[16] Leo Buscaglia (1924-1998) *'Please Listen'* (abridged).

difference? Did the COVID pandemic get in the way (more on this later)?

Alternatively, was treatment delayed because a letter went missing, a phone-call left unanswered, a promise not kept? Were there traumatic experiences on a ward?

Where does that leave you? At best, wary. Can these people upon whom you depend, with 'your life in their hands', be trusted to get it right? Not that, necessarily, you have much choice. Will they tell you the truth? Can you cope with the truth? So how will you find a way of co-operating with professionals, when, really, you're on a 'once-bitten-twice-shy' footing? Maybe it's already too late because trust is broken, whether with professionals, or perhaps life itself. Maybe there's no going back and you never will.

For various reasons then, it may be too late for a cure because a delay has resulted in the cancer only being able to be held at bay or slowed down. Where on earth do you go from there?

A question of compassion

Sometimes patients I see can get past, and even forgive[17], professionals in healthcare for being busy, trying to fix and not listen, and 'dropping the ball'. After all, one frequently leads to another. And we're all human.

But what if that professional, on whose words you hang so much, doesn't even appear to *care*? Thankfully, this seems to me like a rarity and in my experience is something to do with being emotionally exhausted. But once is too often. Where do you go from *there*? For all you may be able to rationalise it, perhaps saying 'they're still a good person, they're just burnt out', that doesn't necessarily help. It's still you on the wrong end of the bad experience.

---

[17] And I'm forever grateful for patients who forgive me. If you're one of them, this footnote is for you!

And people remember what they experience in healthcare; it really matters[18].

Before I go on any further, I would also say *all* professionals can be prone to any number of ways of *not* listening to patients.

Have you tried telling yourself you're being irrational?

Here is another passage[19] that captures common human experiences in situations of suffering:

> *Let us not underestimate how hard it is to listen and be compassionate.*
>
> *Compassion is hard because it requires the inner disposition to go with others where they are weak, vulnerable, lonely and broken. But this is not our spontaneous response to suffering.*

---

[18] For an excellent read on this topic, and how we in healthcare can do better, have a look at Fred Lee's *If Disney Ran Your Hospital: 9 1/2 Things You Would Do Differently* (2005). Second River Healthcare Press: Bozeman.
[19] Nouwen, H.J.M., (1981) *The Way of the Heart: Desert Spirituality and Contemporary Ministry* p. 34. New York: Seabury Press.

What we desire most is to do away with suffering by fleeing from it or finding a quick cure for it. As busy, active, relevant people, we want to earn our bread by making a real contribution. This means first and foremost doing something to show that our presence makes a difference.

And so we ignore our greatest gift, which is our ability to be there, to listen and to enter into solidarity with those who suffer.

Unfortunately, the habit of *not listening* or *not being fully present* is not the exclusive preserve of healthcare settings. The truth is, sometimes the outside world's *not much cop* either. And sometimes this occurs in quite subtle ways....

The wider world: out of the frying pan, into the frying pan...

Not so long ago, people didn't talk publicly about cancer. I remember it; I was there.

Now, you can barely switch on your TV without seeing an appeal for Cancer Research UK, an advert for Macmillan or a storyline in a soap opera. But much as cancer is significantly more visible, our 'folk memory' persists. Cancer is still scary; it is linked to death. It reminds us of our mortality. And so, with the best will in the world, 'Jo(e) Public' doesn't always get it right; sometimes Jo(e) gets it spectacularly wrong. Because it's an emotive subject, people will say all sorts of things to try to (or appear to try to) make the situation better. Whether it's wholeheartedly for the benefit of the patient, or to make themselves feel better, is an interesting point. I suspect the latter in a number of cases. Here are some things I've heard that you, as patients, have heard:

> 'You look well'
> 'Why don't you just...?'
> 'If I were you...'
> 'There's lots of good treatments out there'
> 'Do you know cow's milk is full of hormones?'
> 'Have you heard about the broccoli diet?'
> Etc. *ad nauseam*

This is called by various names, including the *Tyranny of Positive Thinking*[20]. This captures the sense of oppression that can be felt when there is an implied obligation to be positive, to try harder. As the respected BBC journalist Jenni Murray[21] once put it, 'Positive thinking makes me sick!'. If one is not a hero (or at least a trainee-hero), battling away, then the implication is that one is not trying hard enough, or simply enjoying being ill. Or, perhaps, one has brought it on oneself. The underlying moral judgement is clear.

This in itself is not a new story. There's a tale in the Bible about a man called Job, afflicted as he was on many fronts. Fair enough, his friends did sit with him for a number of days and kept their peace, but true to human nature, before long began to advise him of what he needed to do because he was clearly getting it wrong! Here's a modern 'take' on Job:

And this story also nicely illustrates something that's become apparent in many conversations I've had; telling the patients where they're getting it wrong serves a psychological function for the teller.

[20] For example, Coifman, K.G., Flynn, J.J. & Pinto, L.A. (2016) 'When context matters: Negative emotions predict psychological health and adjustment'. Motiv Emot 40, 602–624.

[21] Positive thinking makes me sick: Jenni Murray on why she hates the self-help industry. https://www.dailymail.co.uk/health/article-1247850/ Positive-thinking-makes-sick-JENNI-MURRAY-hates-self-help-industry.html#ixzz 4am4rCZac (accessed July 2020)

'It won't happen to me because I have done it / would do it differently ... and he's a sinner[22] anyway, not like me....' No wonder the unfortunate Job felt so miserable.... as if his many afflictions weren't bad enough, his 'comforters' made him feel worse![23]

... 'how are you?'

As you'll have gathered, I tend to get my best ideas from my patients. This is another one. I once met this lady[24] who had caught on quite quickly regarding how to field enquiries. She'd realised being asked 'how are you?' was often-times more of a polite enquiry rather than an invitation for an authentic answer[25]. It was, even at times, the very opposite; an indication that the enquirer was hoping for an up-beat response. *Her* response, she told me was generally:

> Would you like the short or the long answer?

Having said that... **being positive, and encouraging others to be, isn't (necessarily) a negative.**

In fact, the consensus increasingly states that positivity is good for your health. I won't get into the 'mind/body' debate, the cul-de-sac about whether your mind 'influences' your body or the other way round... the very language we use betrays a certain 'dualism[26]' which

---

[22] Contemporary equivalents—'unmotivated', 'loser', 'mood hoover' etc.

[23] Spoiler alert: in the end they get shown up and he is vindicated. For people of faith, and maybe those who aren't, the story has a helpful spiritual message, offering some thoughts around the ultimate question 'why do bad things happen to good people?'

[24] She preferred the designation 'lady' to 'woman' in case that matters to you.

[25] You may have heard this one... Q: 'What's the biggest lie told in church?' A: 'I'm fine thanks'

[26] If you've got nothing better to do, look up Descartes (1596-1650) who wondered how we experience pain, given that it appears to be a physical stimulus (e.g., fire) that triggers a 'mental' experience (i.e., 'ow!'). He wondered whether a little bell might be ringing in the brain.

would be alien to some traditional Asian philosophies. What seems to be clear enough is that a 'positive' mindset seems to be associated with a better immune system[27]. Even if you don't happen to believe that the mind can directly influence the wellbeing of the body, it makes sense really; getting stuck in, as one[28] might call it, means doing things that are good for you, rather than by choice crawling into a safe but depressing shell. Conversely, being 'stressed out' with ruminations of negative thoughts like worries because one never breaks the pattern by going out, when done as a long-term habit, has been linked with higher cortisol[29], which apparently is bad news for the health. So, the bottom line is that, yes, being positive is good, as much as you can be, but it needs to be *your* positivity and done when *you're* ready—and that only tends to emerge when you feel well and truly listened to.

So far, we've devoted a bit of space to 'listening' to your experiences of professionals and the wider public; maybe it's a good moment now to come closer to home...

And what do you make of it all...what is your story?

...'bad luck'

We all know it, don't we? Stuff[30] happens. I began writing this about four months after the UK's COVID lockdown began. The reality is that cancer diagnostics and treatment have been delayed, with a great deal of NHS resources poured into crisis-management. On top of this, many potential patients have been quite understandably reluctant to come forward to their GPs for fear of becoming COVID-infected or wasting the doctor's time (assuming they could have secured an

---

[27] A chance to use a long word here; the field of science is called.... deep breath....'Psychoneuroimmunology'. You may wish to visit https://www.uq.edu.au/news/article/2014/09/positive-boost-immune-system (accessed 10/06/2022)

[28] Alright, as *I* would call it

[29] For example, https://www.nhs.uk/news/mental-health/stress-and-heart-attacks/ (accessed 10/06/2022, subsequently 'retired')

[30] Another chance to insert your favourite 4-letter word

appointment of course). In the UK, urgent cancer treatment was down by 60% in April 2020[31] and the media has plenty of stories about delayed tests/treatment[32]. Much of this is nobody's fault. But it has psychological consequences. What will it feel like to be told, 'I'm sorry, the cancer's too advanced, we're looking at keeping it under control not taking it away'? What will it be like for the professionals having to break this news for that matter?

What impact do these sorts of situations, which although nobody's fault, have on you? We may know 'stuff happens', but do we really *accept* it? Or did we at some level always think 'the bullet's got someone else's name on it'…it won't happen to me. But then, when it does, where do we go from there?

I've heard various versions of 'this should not have happened, it's not the life I had in mind'. You may have worked hard for many years and five minutes after you retire you get a diagnosis. Or you may have young children.

It's not unusual at that point to embark on a retrospective search for reasons, and sometimes we find out what we really believe; e.g. 'I've always been a good person … not like … [insert group of people who deserve bad things to happen to them]'. We tend to believe bad things happen to bad people, not good[33], and 'you make your own luck'. After all, you've spent some serious time in the gym, or eaten lots of broccoli. You can't have lung cancer, you've never smoked (or gave up years ago).

There are undoubtedly whole books written about this stuff[34]; why people look for medical and moral causes when the diagnosis

---

[31] Clover, B (2020) 'Urgent cancer treatment down 60 per cent in April'. Health Service Journal. 11/06/2020.

[32] For example, Sunday Times 05/04/2020.

[33] Known by academics as the 'Just World Hypothesis'.

[34] For the interested, you may wish to read Elisabeth Kubler-Ross' work on stages of coming to terms with a diagnosis: *On Death and Dying* (2008) Abingdon: Routledge.

happens to them[35]. My hunch is that there is a comfort in restoring a sense of order, in predictability, in 'this-causes-that' thinking because, however uncomfortable our conclusions may be as to why it has happened to us, it's better than no conclusions, and gives us something we can work on. For these reasons, for most people, 'bad luck' just doesn't cut it...

...'this wasn't in the plan'...

Your plan   Your reality

Staying with the pain?

Where do you go from there, if anywhere at all?

Do you stay with a 'thanks, but no thanks' stance to the life that turns out to be on offer, as opposed to the one you had in mind? I call this *'brassed off syndrome'*[36]. If that's 'where you're at', I would not judge you for it. That's not my place; if I were to judge, I would

---

[35] Interestingly, I've noticed on my travels that some cultures, such as in Ghana, do have a way of explaining misfortune along the lines of 'someone's got it in for me'. As I understand it, such beliefs persist, albeit more under the surface these days. My guess is that may serve a useful psychological function for the sufferer.

[36] Well, that's the cleaned-up version. And, yes, a little bit pretentious of me, I'll admit. Just shorthand really. Insoo Kim Berg, one of the founders of the solution-focused practice, might call this the 'complainant' position: Berg, I. K. (1989). 'Of visitors, complainants, and customers: Is there really such a thing as "resistance?"' Family Therapy Networker, 13(1): 21.

become part of the problem rather than the solution. In these situations, in this book, just as in an appointment, I would say... 'maybe that's enough for now'. Read on when you're ready. In an appointment, I might say 'is this as far as you want to go for the foreseeable; will it be enough to have vented today... or are you hoping for more? Would you be pleased to see signs of you even minimally dealing better with life? If so, let's keep talking'.

Similarly, if you're ready, read on. If not, that's also OK. Maybe re-read this chapter. Just come back when ready...

Summing it up: timing is everything...

Speaking of choosing the right moment to engage with change and the importance of being prepared to 'sit with the sh*t' in the meantime, here is *something I prepared earlier* that encompasses the typical sequence of events in an appointment[37]:

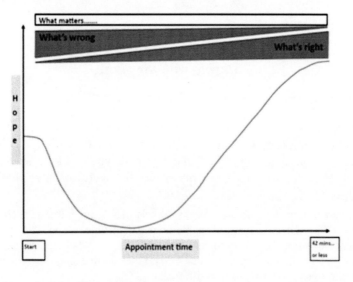

---

[37] If you're looking for a learned academic reference in this footnote, there isn't one. I 'drew' this graph one day on my laptop to capture the typical choreography of a few thousand appointments I have been involved in during my work as a clinical psychologist.

Typically, during the early part of an appointment (which usually lasts 42 minutes), especially a first one, whilst listening out for what matters[38] to the patient, and what's right[39] in their world, I hear a lot about *what's wrong*, as represented by the top left of the blue area. Fair enough… it's their chance to be heard, especially if, in the manner described above, they haven't been particularly well listened to by professionals or wider society! Or, indeed, if they've had way more than their fair share of 'bad luck'. As you'll see, the red line goes down as, for a time, the sense of hope in the room (mine as much as theirs) drops. Actually, maybe it's largely mine… People at some level know another story about themselves, have some sense of their own resilience, even if the right moment in the appointment hasn't yet arrived when they're ready to share this alternative story. As you can also see, the curve *does* turn upwards, but more of that in later chapters. The most important point for now is that this is their 'day in court', and it does no harm for me to feel a little of what they feel[40]. And, for that matter, one should not 'signpost' to other services prematurely because of being busy or out of a need to 'do' something.

And the conversation will move on when it's ready…

Stick or twist?

So… have you felt listened to so far? Some sense of 'I (me, Dominic) get where you're at?' If so, when you've had a cup of tea[41], you might want to read on. You may even want to jump to Chapter three if you want to get straight down to business, to get working on your future life. If you're *not* ready to read on, maybe reflect to yourself, 'maybe

---

[38] Much more of this in Chapter 3.

[39] Much more of this in Chapter 4.

[40] After I'd written this, I heard Tony Hawks talk about 'Nonviolent Communication (NVC)', which has been described thus: "When we focus on clarifying what is being observed, felt and needed rather than on diagnosing and judging, we discover the depth of our own compassion"; Rosenberg, M.B. Nonviolent Communication: A Language of Life, 3rd edition (2015) Encinitas (USA): Puddledancer Press, p. 3

[41] Other beverages are available…

I just need to lick my wounds for a bit…. I'll come back to this book if/when ready'. Maybe you're already thinking of better uses for it, like a doorstop or a fire-lighter…

Or, if you do want to read on, but are wondering *why* you seem to be not quite yourself while the rest of the world carries on, have a look at Chapter two…

CHAPTER TWO

YOU ARE NOT ALONE; EXPERIENCES OF 'BEING IN THE SAME BOAT'

Chapter summary:

'Actually, no, you're probably *not* losing the plot'

- Examples of typical lived experiences of cancer;
- A little bit of explanation for them;
- Some more long words.

More often than not, and sooner rather than later in an appointment, it becomes apparent that the patient has a sense of losing themselves; they're not only noticing weird stuff happening, but they're becoming concerned about it. Their lived experience[42], frequently of anxiety regarding cancer recurrence, its effect on their family, etc, is compounded by an anxiety about the out-workings of their anxiety.

You may well ask: *What does all that mean*?

Well, it's not unusual for people to tell me they're losing their memory. They forget where they leave things, whatever they've just read[43], even their train of thought. Alongside that, they lose their confidence; in going out and about, especially to busy or public

---

[42] This is a chapter about the phenomenology of cancer. There's no particular reason for this footnote other than to use a long word to impress any professionals who might still be reading by this point…

[43] This is one of my excuses for writing a briefer-than-averagebook.

places[44]. They lose their confidence in their ability to make decisions and frequently their confidence in the future. On top of all that, and maybe worst of all, they start noticing, really noticing, all sorts of aches, pains and other bodily sensations they wouldn't have given the time of day to in their pre-cancer life. Ah yes, that time long, long ago when things were so much better. This is not necessarily even an exhaustive list.

Let me expand on some of these things. I won't go on too long; there are other, inside-story autobiographies out there that speak eloquently, and I don't want to accentuate the negative or to lower the mood more than is necessary or get repetitive.

A question of remembering[45]

If you're 'in the thick of it' as you read this, then you may be struggling to absorb the text, although that may be something to do with my writing style. Alternatively, and I would like to think this is more likely, it could be because you're finding everything difficult to 'process' at the moment. I've seen this many times with folks I've met. *War and Peace*[46]? No chance. A modern novel? Unlikely. *Chat* magazine? That's more like it. I once met a chap who would normally read *The Liverpool Echo.* His 'starting point', post-diagnosis, was just the headlines. On a good day[47].

Basically, what psychologists tend to call your 'short-term memory' isn't working well. This is probably why you lose your thread in

---

[44] The real definition of agoraphobia, by the way, which comes from *agora*, Greek for 'gathering space'. It's not to do with 'agriculture' so it's not really about fields or open spaces. I note this in case it's useful, hopefully not to show off. Too much…

[45] Some people attribute these signs/symptoms to 'chemobrain' but the truth is they also occur in people who haven't had it so the biomedical effects of chemotherapy cannot be the whole story.

[46] This gives me an opportunity to mention casually that I have read it. And *Lord of the Rings.* But not a lot else.

[47] Spoiler alert; he worked his way up from that and did OK. But he had to start very small.

conversation and forget where you put your keys (etc.). Because, most likely, your mind's not quite on the job, for good reasons (see below). I know for myself if I have to retain something, I have to pay attention[48], which often amounts to mulling on something, and making an effort to remember it[49]. One way of doing this consciously[50], or sometimes unconsciously, is to associate whatever one is trying to remember with something that is already well remembered or noticed in the environment in some kind of 'mental journey'[51], like tying a knot in a later-to-be-retrieved hankie, but mentally[52]. However, if one isn't fully concentrating, this is less likely to happen.

A question of confidence

As I write this, many people are subject to the 'lockdown' part of the COVID-19 response. By the time you read it, all being well, this will be in the past. But you may yet remember, whether you have had cancer or not, what it was like suddenly to confront the world again; surprisingly daunting. Right now, I'm doing a fair few telephone appointments and a number of people who have or have had cancer have shared variations of 'I suppose I shouldn't be saying this… but I'm sort of glad that we're all in the same boat, I don't stand out now, other people know what it's like'.

This sense of being daunted seems to be a common feature of post-diagnosis life, particularly when the initial treatments are done-and-dusted. There comes at a time when others expect the individual with cancer to come out of their particular 'cocoon'; when their nearest-

---

[48] I'm hoping my wife isn't reading this.

[49] No, I'm *really* hoping my wife isn't reading this.

[50] I'm using these terms colloquially here; no reference to psycho-analytic theory intended, mainly because I don't understand it.

[51] The ancient Greeks thought of this first, like lots of psychological things; for example, in a legal trial remembering the sequence of an alleged murder by envisioning daggers growing on a tree. For a better explanation, see https://www.britannica.com/topic/mnemonic (accessed 10/06/2022)

[52] Another useful sort of mnemonic, in case useful, is rhyme; for example, 'divorced, beheaded, died…divorced, beheaded, survived' (which pertains to Henry VIII, if you haven't heard it before)

and-dearest want to have a party and are expecting, or some could say prescribing, positivity (see the *Tyranny of Positive Thinking* section in Chapter 1).

But, of course, by its very nature, a cocoon, like the 'lockdown', is simultaneously constraining and *safe*. My 'take' on the phenomenology[53] of this is that there are three sets of reasons why people feel safe in their cocoon, and correspondingly unsafe when it's time to leave it.

Firstly, modern treatment tends to follow diagnosis very quickly, thanks[54] to cancer targets. There is no time to 'draw breath', in modern parlance. Before you know it, you are getting prepped for an operation, tattooed and bombarded with information[55]. Swept off your feet and not for romantic reasons. You have a whole new career, or at least occupation: cancer patient. Welcome to your new life. You embark on 'ticking treatments off the list'; 'how many chemos to go?' etc. People begin to rally round; the classic 'if there's anything I can do' emerges and, often, your nearest-and-dearest may begin to cosset you.

If I may digress for a paragraph, this cosseting may yet be a two-edged sword. Yes, for many it's lovely to be looked after. But then… at what cost? Does a person lose their very sense of self? The one who is the 'go-to' pillar of the family may become the person whom now nobody asks for advice. Or more practically, the one who runs

---

[53] I felt it was time for a long word again as I was offering a theory. In this context, it means 'lived experience'.

[54] I use the word ambiguously. For many, quick treatment is a good thing from a medical outcome point of view. But this isn't always the case: I've seen situations where the target is the priority, where medical benefit of fast-tracking is marginal at best; the preference/overall wellbeing of the patient is not the deciding factor.

[55] By the by, I read many years ago that at an appointment when the diagnosis is given, patients can only remember one word. Cancer. For example, see M. van Osch et al. (2014) 'Reducing patients' anxiety and uncertainty, and improving recall in bad news consultations'. *Health Psychology*, 33(11), 1382–1390. https://doi.org/10.1037/hea0000097 (accessed 10/06/2022)

the show at home may be no longer able to carry out these tasks. I've lost count of the number of women who've told me their husband doesn't hang bedsheets up properly to dry; an instant 'downer' for the woman and, sometimes, a cause of conflict.

Secondly, the very process of treatment has significance; 'something is being done'. It's so much easier for the patient (and their loved ones) to cope with a scary experience by having that sense of reassurance. Some patients I have known have really 'gone to town' with this concept, essentially by making a story out of what's happening during treatment[56]. One woman I met during chemo imagined a Red Army[57] getting into every nook and cranny inside her to blow away cancer cells; another with lung cancer would imagine the 'jellyfish' in her chest being pierced every time she had an injection, and, just for good measure, she would sometimes beat her chest herself.

Thirdly, surveillance is a great thing when we are scared. During cancer treatment, as intense as the experience might be, the patient has the reassurance of frequent appointments with experts keeping an eye on them. This may be through the informal 'how are you', or in the course of scans and examinations etc. And, of course, all along, the built-in supportive warmth that many health professionals just do as 'standard' is present.

Hence, at the end of intense treatments, the patient, having not really had much time to 'catch up' with what's just happened, is 'left' to get on with their life without the support to which they've become accustomed. They're required to 'stand on their own two feet' at a time when they are most psychologically vulnerable. This process, I would suggest, is akin to what was seen when many long-term psychiatric and similar hospitals were closed[58] in the UK and the

---

[56] Yes, in psychological circles, this has a name, the narrative approach; hence in Narrative Therapy, patients are invited to generate a story, or amplify an existing one, for example concerning a fight with an alien invader, naturally with a successful outcome.

[57] Her chemo was apparently red.

[58] Known as *deinstitutionalisation.*

Western world. People whose whole world had been within them were then encouraged to engage with the outside world. A similar situation can also be seen when service people with many years in the armed forces behind them re-join civilian life.

No wonder then that the everyday tasks requiring getting out and about, such as shopping, not to mention social expectations such as baptisms, weddings, funerals, parties and family gatherings become small mountains to climb. Having been 'shielded' from routine, everyday challenges and the opportunity to experience dealing well with them, everything consequently feels like a significant obstacle. And scary… which leads on to:

A question of (hyper) vigilance

Have you heard about a guy called Damocles and his sword?

The story goes[59], that a traveller in 4th century BC Sicily, seeking favour with the despot Dionysius II, expressed admiration for his position and was duly invited to sit on the king's throne. All was good until Damocles chanced to look up and saw an uncomfortably large and sharp sword hanging over him dubiously, held only by a single horse hair that could snap at any time; a reminder for Dionysius, to himself apparently, of how precarious his position was.

This pithy observation of how tenuous life can be has passed into cancer literature as the Damocles Syndrome[60] . Essentially, to you and me, that's the sense of one's own mortality that people seem to acquire after a diagnosis.

---

[59] Attributed to Timaeus of Tauromenium (c. 356–260 BC)
[60] For example, Curda, A. 'The Damocles Syndrome: Where We Are Today'. *J Canc Educ* 26, 397–398 (2011).

Here's another way of looking at it.

Imagine you are a young gazelle on the African savannah without a care in the world; nothing much of great consequence has yet happened to you. Your life consists largely of grazing on grass, playing and sleeping. Then one day, a lion comes along out of the blue and eats your best friend. From now on, you are going to be more vigilant. Much more vigilant. You are not just looking out for lions, but anything yellow, the movement of grass, especially at the time of day that the incident happened[61]. And as soon as anything of that ilk occurs, the *fight or flight* response is frequently triggered. With fighting probably not being a great option in this instance, you'll run. Running means that your heart rate will increase to get blood to your muscles, you'll hyperventilate to get oxygen into that blood, pant to get rid of excess heat, your digestive system will close down as blood is diverted, you may be sick and your mouth will dry[62]. You'll certainly not be sleeping.

---

[61] This is known as *generalization*.

[62] Interestingly (at least I think so), this formed the basis of early lie detection. The accused had a mouthful of dry rice and, after a while, if it remained dry, they were deemed guilty and executed! See for example

Do any of those sound familiar to you? That's what the bodily signs and symptoms of anxiety are[63]. On the most basic level, anxiety is a good thing as, in the story of our gazelle, it enables you to stay alive and avoid the lion coming to get you. This natural reaction is really helpful in short bursts, making the body react rapidly. It gets you out of a fix, and helps you perform when you need to[64]. But it can be exhausting. While short bursts of anxiety can be manageable, and even helpful to getting things done, too much can be overwhelming and certainly debilitating.

With particular reference to hypervigilance, that is, an *excess* of vigilance, perhaps a more day-to-day example for us humans would be out on the road. Supposing you've done your homework and had decided to buy a particular type or colour of car. Have you ever had the experience of suddenly seeing them everywhere? Still more so if you have been in an accident; once I was asked to see a woman recovering from cancer who told me how she'd sometime before been driving along and, without warning, a red car came out of a side-road and hit her. Once she'd eventually plucked up the courage to get back on the road, she'd spent months afterwards catching sight of red cars[65].

In a similar way to my patient's awareness of red cars, due to hypervigilance, you'll likely find that TV, newspapers, magazines and billboards are suddenly full of adverts for cancer charities or cancer stories. You'll notice cancer in friends and family, however distantly related. It will seem like the world has changed overnight.

For some cancer experiences—for example people who have or had a blood cancer diagnosis—this hypervigilance thing can be particularly tricky. Why? Because for some of them they did not have noticeable symptoms and their blood cancer was picked up by chance. In this case, there is the added worry of not knowing what

---

Vicianova, M (2015) 'Historical Techniques of Lie Detection', *Eur J Psychol.* Aug; 11(3): 522–534.

[63] With the obvious exception of panting to lose heat; we sweat to do that.

[64] Anecdotally, many stage performers I believe say this.

[65] More on this story later.

they are looking for. If nothing is a clear sign of danger, then potentially everything is.

Sometimes, hypervigilance not only leads us to noticing more instances of the feared object; without meaning to, it can greatly magnify the imagined *size* of the problem. Most of us have had the experience of feeling a hole in our gum where a tooth used to be; it can seem like a crater! It's like that. In fact, one man I was asked to see had actually had mouth cancer and he really struggled to move his focus away from what was going on in there; the slightest (perceived) change would send him into a tailspin. This is a particular example of what we all know as being anxious. It can take on a whole life of its own and become an unwanted habit...

Being anxious about being anxious

Let's reflect on things for a moment.

When you notice what could be a lump, pain, fatigue, or even an advert on the TV, what commonly happens? As often as not, your 'fight-or-flight' response kicks in. As if we're about to run away from the lion or a similar threat, our bodies 'gear up'. That spurt of adrenaline, tightening of the chest, the knot in the stomach, and before we know it, we're ready for action. All revved up with no place to go[66]. So what's happened? You've got too much oxygen in your blood with a sense of light-headed 'swimmyness' and your brain doesn't like it; you might even get blurred vision. You notice these weird sensations and worry some more. You see where this is going? In the 'old days', when people got 'into a state', they were encouraged to breathe in and out whilst applying a paper bag to their mouth; this was effective in re-balancing the blood-borne carbon

---

[66] Meatloaf/Steinman *All Revved Up with No Place to Go* lyrics © 1977 Round Hill Music Big Loud Songs, Carlin America Inc. from the album *Bat out of Hell*.

dioxide. As it happens, controlled breathing[67] does the same thing. But *what do you already know* about calming yourself down[68]?

Similarly, if we think about it, what do we often notice when our muscles are tensed, as if ready to run or fight? If we do it for long enough, or frequently enough, quite possibly *pain.* You can see where this is going; completely without meaning to, we generate the symptom we're most frightened of. And it may come in more subtle forms. Suppose your voice goes hoarse? Is this a recurrence of cancer, or as is likely when we're anxious, a tightening of the vocal cords? And there are many ways to relax our bodies; many books and online resources. Once again, *what do you already know* about what works for you[6970]?

A question of 'stages'

Kubler-Ross, as mentioned earlier[71], had some very helpful things to say about typical reactions to living with a long-term condition. Lots about denial, anger, renegotiation and acceptance. Although often quoted, these "stages" were never meant to be a "set" sequence of things that people do. On many occasions, the lived experience is more circular in nature, but these are good descriptors of the various emotions experienced in varying amounts over the course of time.

So, you might find this model helpful if you are the sort of person who likes to put a name to an experience, even if it only therefore

---

[67] For example, breathe in for a slow count of 6, pause for 6, and let the breath out for 10 through pursed lips. Repeat this until you feel calm. But if you'd like more specific advice, there are plenty of self-help books full of ideas in many good bookshops!

[68] More in chapter 4 on the topic of your expertise!

[69] More in chapter 4 on the topic of your expertise!

[70] If the symptoms I talk of persist, obviously get them checked out.

[71] For example, *On Death and Dying* (2008) Abingdon: Routledge.

suggests that other people have experienced the same sorts of things[72].

One particular 'stage' I see a lot of is anger. As we saw in Chapter 1, this isn't always in the obvious way of 'why has this happened to *me*?'. It's more along the lines of 'this wasn't what I planned', 'I feel trapped', 'done to'… leading to the fight/flight instinct I talked about earlier. This is often accompanied by an element of 'if only'… in the form of wishing one could go back in a time machine to a better, typically idealised, version of the past. Just as everything else in an appointment, these thoughts and feelings still need to be aired and listened to.

Don't Panic Mr Mainwaring[73]

So here's the good news: the bottom line is these human experiences mentioned in this chapter are normal and are to be expected. If you can help it, don't beat yourself up for how you feel about your situation. You're not the first and you won't be the last.

Don't be anxious about being anxious. A bit of anxiety is healthy; it keeps you watching out for lions, or, in this context, it keeps you watching out for signs and symptoms that you should get checked out[74].

---

[72] And at least you can impress people with your deep knowledge of psychology.

[73] For people of a non-British disposition, this is a reference to a much-loved catchphrase of Corporal Jones in a classic TV/radio sitcom about the WWII Home Guard called *Dad's Army*. The best line of all appeared in an episode entitled *The Deadly Attachment* (1973): [U-Boat captain to platoon member singing derisory song] 'Your name will also go on the list…what is it?' [Mainwaring, the platoon captain] 'Don't tell him Pike!'. Catch it on YouTube… laughter is therapeutic; this might be the best thing you get out of this book.

[74] I'm not even going to begin to list them here; that's outside my competence. The NHS website is a great place to start: https://www.nhs.uk/.

It also reminds you that one day, you will die, as we all will[75]. Death and taxes and all that.

This in turn, implies your mission, *should you choose to accept it*[76]*;* that is, given that you now have a first-hand experience of your mortality, *what are you going to do to make the very most of being alive?*

Are you ready to read on?

Much more on this in Chapter 3.

---

[75] Remember that you are absolutely unique. Just like everyone else. (Often attributed to Margaret Meade.)
[76] Mission: Impossible. CBS Television 1966 onward. I actually do say this to patients. The point is, it's not my life to direct. And people seldom used to do the 'homework' I suggested so I stopped doing setting it!

CHAPTER THREE

CANCER.
THE END…
OR A NEW BEGINNING?

'On their death-bed, no-one ever said *'I wish I'd spent more time in the office'*'[77]

Chapter summary: • Powerful questions that uncover new lives; • Examples of 'made-to-measure' new lives, lasting five days or fifty years; • Some more long words and another poem.

To begin at the beginning[78]

…is the obvious thing to do. After all, what can we know of life in the future?[79] And yet… one definition of insanity is: doing the same thing and expecting a different result[80]. Maybe it's time to do something different. Be radical. Ready?

Tell me what you want, what you really, really, want[81]…

---

[77] Rabbi Harold Kushner (1935-)

[78] Dylan Thomas (1954) *Under Milk Wood.* BBC Radio Production.

[79] Other than it has likely, by the very fact of you reading this book, had some nasty surprises so tends to do that?

[80] Attributed to Einstein, although, apparently, he didn't quite say that.

[81] Spice Girls (1996) - Wannabe. © Sony/ATV Music Publishing LLC, Universal Music Publishing Group, Peermusic Publishing

…alternatively, 'if you don't know where the hole is, it's going to be a long day on the golf course![82]'

Of course I have an agenda, because starting with the future and working backwards is what solution-focused (SF) conversations are built on. This is, unsurprisingly, called establishing the *preferred future.* And there is a particularly good reason for being future-focused; often as not it works better than being mired in a bog of impossibility and anxiety[83]. Given that you've got through Chapters 1 and 2, or have jumped straight to 3 and are reading this, which is the literary equivalent of still being in the appointment room, I'm going to assume you're at least prepared to give it a go! I'm going to take you through some questions I (and other SF practitioners) often ask and show how the conversation tends to develop from them. But rather than privilege my questions by putting them first, let's hear the patient's voice…

---

[82] Hoyt, M. (1996) *A Golfer's Guide to Brief Therapy* in Constructive Therapies 2. Guildford Press.

[83] If you'd like to know a lot more about the philosophy of SF thought and how it contrasts, for example with 'classical' CBT, see chapter 5.

Straight from the heart

Every now and then, someone who meets with me really 'goes for it' when I ask them anything about what they want. So, let's start there[84]. Straight-faced, they ask to come back with something like:

"Seeing as you ask, can you cure my cancer?" or "Can I have a one-way ticket to Switzerland[85]?"

Presumably at this point, I would either, in the case of the former be expected to run out of the room to fetch an oncologist to (re)break the bad news or in the case of the latter, fetch a psychiatrist (more on that a bit later).

Neither of which I actually do[86].

Instead, this is a *golden* opportunity to hear what really matters to the patient... yes, what they really, *really* want.

So, where does the conversation go from there?

Tread softly[87]

Regarding the wish for a cure (I'll come back to the Switzerland scenario below), it's fairly standard practice, as I've gathered, having

---

[84] As well as starting with the patient voice, it's also a strategic move to cover this first in case any of my professional colleagues are still reading at this point. Almost without exception, when I'm offering a bit of SF training, someone will fold their arms and say 'but what if the patient wants something that's impossible?!'. By tackling this issue now, hopefully not only will it make the book more engaging for everybody else, it might keep the sceptics reading!

[85] Yes, someone really did say that. In case you didn't get it, it's a reference to Dignitas.

[86] I hope this is not out of hubris but because I believe more good can be done by staying in.

[87] W. B. Yeats (1865-1939): 'But I, being poor, have only my dreams; I have spread my dreams under your feet; Tread softly because you tread on my dreams', from his love poem *The Cloths of Heaven* to Maud Gonne, who never consented to marry him.

discussed this issue many times with medical colleagues, to come back with:

"Ah yes, that would be lovely, but can you talk about something a little bit more realistic?"

…which is good as far as it goes. But if you think about it, there is an inherent shaping of the conversation by the professional, which immediately means they are taking control. Perhaps it is born of an mistrust of the patient; it implies 'talk of a cure is off limits because there needs to be no room for any misunderstanding and no chance you will run away with *false hope*'. You can see how there is an implied paternalism. It's an elaborate 'yes…but'. It is also potentially a trampling on dreams, which is going to hurt and do nothing for the all-important therapeutic relationship[88].

What is false hope anyway? This is surely, to a degree, in the eye of the beholder. Though, in a sense, hope is hope is hope; it doesn't necessarily have to have a specific outcome. To quote a much-loved hymn 'Strength for today, and *bright hope for tomorrow*'[89] The writer doesn't say hope for *what* exactly; singers of the hymn just 'get it'. It doesn't need to be spelled out. Are they inspired and does it make a difference to what happens next, including their health? You wouldn't bet against it…

…and respecting the dream

So, as you've gathered, I'm not a fan of the above approach. It's a reasonable question though; *is* there another option? Even one that

---

[88] People have written whole books on that subject. Suffice it to say the quality of any therapeutic relationship, particularly as regards talking therapies, is the biggest predictor of therapeutic success, not the model per se; see Smith, M. L., Glass, G. V., & Miller, T. I. (1980). *The benefits of psychotherapy*. Baltimore, MD: John Hopkins University Press.

[89] Thomas Chisholm (1866–1960) *Great Is Thy Faithfulness*. Pub. 1923 by Hope Publishing Carol Stream: IL.

brings us back to our mission, to be excited about what the patient is excited about, truly respecting their dream?

I think there is. Taking up from just before where we left off:

P (as in **P**atient): *Seeing as you ask, can you cure my cancer?*

H (as in **H**elpful Person[90]): Right! Of course, that's what you'd want! Why wouldn't you? [pause to give extra respect to the dream[91]] and if your cancer was cured, what difference would that make to you?

P: …Well…I wouldn't be like this. In pain all the time… never stopping thinking about cancer[92]… I'd be me again….

H: Hmmmm… ah, got it… tell me all about being you again… who would notice that had happened?

P: Uh…dunno… er… well I'd stop feeling useless… I'd be involved again….

H: Right… and who might be the first to notice you getting involved again…?[93]

Hopefully you can see where the above sequence is going, one I have been involved in many times. Sometimes the beginning is not so dramatic as 'a wish for a cure', but the process often becomes the

---

[90] Apologies for the clumsy terminology. I'm trying to cover all the possibilities; to be an effective SF question-asker, you don't necessarily need to be a 'therapist'.

[91] …and to see if the patient has fallen off their chair in surprise at not being 'managed' back into reality.

[92] When you ask what people want, very usually they start telling you what their problems are; in effect, what they don't want. However, if you're prepared to stick with it, the 'preferred future' does generally emerge, as in this example.

[93] Prof. Deborah Christie commented when reviewing an earlier manuscript: [it] reminds me of a kid with a [cancer] I worked with whose miracle was to be a professional footballer - the MDT (Multidisciplinary Team] told me I had to talk him out of it … of course I didn't and he ended up becoming a disabled athlete.

same. A 'journey[94]' from 'Impossibility Land[95]' to the land of 'Maybe, just Maybe' has begun. Hope is re-kindled as the glimmerings of self-belief[96] are created[97].

Listen hard… and when it's really bad, listen harder

Coming back to the 'one way ticket to Switzerland' situation, this happens in various guises fairly frequently in my appointments. Maybe I just depress people when they first clap eyes on me. Or maybe I just look like I *do* want to hear the whole story.

For me, when, straight from the heart people talk of death being preferable to their situation, it's a cue for some extra listening. Listening rather than reacting is likely to be the most helpful thing right there and then; hence, I ask another question. Perhaps I better stress at this point that I will always see these conversations through to a point where the person has credible alternatives to self-harm, as described below. If (very rarely) that doesn't happen and the person is still at risk, I will put the usual safeguarding measures in place.

So, resuming from where we left off:

P: *Can I have a one-way ticket to Switzerland?* or even *I'd rather be dead.*

H: You must have good reasons for saying that. What would be better if that happened?

P: Well, I wouldn't be in pain or sick or worried any more…

---

[94] Semi-apologies for using the modern cliché of being 'on a journey', much beloved, for example, of celebrities tracing their colourful ancestors on reality TV shows. It just seems to fit here.

[95] I've nicked that metaphor from the title of a SF book by O'Hanlon, B and Beadle, S. (2000) *A Field Guide to Possibility Land.* BT Press: London.

[96] For the interested, these are thoughts called 'secondary appraisals'. As usual, I'm throwing that term in there to claim a veneer of academic respectability.

[97] This may be an appalling case of mixing my metaphors

H: Right... of course...and what difference would that make to you?

P: I'd be more like myself again.

H: I haven't met you 'til today... what would your old self be like if we'd met then?

P: Good company, feeling useful, not like this.

H: What would it mean to you to be more like your old self, good company, useful, I guess involved in things?

P: That would be amazing... but I can't see it happening.

H: Hmmmmm...who would be the least surprised if it did happen?

P: ... My best friend Sam...she keeps telling me she believes in me.

H: What has Sam noticed in you before that makes her think that?

P: She says I'm strong... I suppose because I got through a horrible divorce.

H: Right...so what did that take...

As hopefully is fairly clear from the sequence above, which is representative of many such conversations, by offering an ear, as opposed to a closing-down reactive approach, an opportunity is created for hope to be rediscovered.

Here is a variation on that sequence that can also occur:

P: *Can I have a one-way ticket to Switzerland?* or even *I'd rather be dead.*

H: You must have good reasons for saying that. What would be better if that happened?

P: Well, I wouldn't be in pain or sick or worried any more...

H: Right.... of course... and what difference would that make to you?

P: I dunno… it's just Groundhog Day every day for me, there is nothing to live for!

H: Ah…right… [pause]… so what *does* it take to keep going at all?

P: It's really hard... sometimes I don't even bother getting up.

H: What does it take to get through *those* days?

P: I just sleep a lot so I don't have to face things

H: Does that work for you?

P: Yes… but then I'm wasting my life anyway.

H: From what you've shared, it sounds like some days you *do* get up… is that slightly less bad than staying in bed, a bit less of a waste?

P: Yes, but I don't do it very often.

H: Understood. And to make sure I'm properly 'getting what you're saying', life's really tough so you spend a lot of time in bed sleeping the time away as that's the best you can do on those days… and sometimes you do get up which is slightly less bad?

P: Yes.

H: So, what *does it take* to get out of bed?

P: A lot. Usually if I have to do something… like getting some dog food… and I have to let my dog out of course into the garden.

H: What's your dog called?

P: Lola… L-O-L-A, Lola [with the slightest hint of a smile at the musical reference].

H: What sort is she?

P: She's a Cavachon. Thinks she's a princess.

H: Is she quite smart then?

A: Yes, she knows how to get what she wants.

H: So, if I could talk to Lola, what would she say about you?

P: She'd say I was soft and I will always do for her what I won't do for myself.

H: What else do you do for her then?

P: Well I spoil her and always make sure she gets the really expensive dog food they advertise on the telly. I let her sit on me; she's good that way, she knows when I'm feeling low… I shouldn't admit this but she sleeps on the pillow next to me.

A: So you find it in yourself to do quite a lot for her?

P: Yes, I wouldn't want to let her down.

H: Right…. so… how would L-O-L-A Lola know this appointment had done you some good?

P: Er… well… we'd spend more time in the garden together; she's quite a lazy princess but she loves it when I throw a ball for her…

H: How many times do you throw it?

P: On a bad day once or twice…

H: And what would she hope for?

P: That I just did it, say 6 or 7 times.

H: How confident do you feel that's gonna happen?

P: Pretty confident… I owe it to her.

H: Say on a scale of one to ten?

P: Seven or eight.

H: Wow… what makes it that?

P: Well, like I said I owe it to her. And when I make a promise I keep it…

I have just the thing for you Mrs Smith

The appointment continues by exploring what else gives that sense of confidence and what else the patient would like to emerge after the appointment. All of this leads to a sense of a hope, through belief in self, and future plans, including the possibility of a further appointment if needed. The aim is to open up other viable futures than self-destruction.

Yet more on listening to what people want. Including some questions I use to find out someone's preferred future, and some common answers.

(i) 'Nuclear' questions.

I call them that as, being highly emotive, they aren't necessarily a strategy that would be my 'go-to' with everyone, and usually not early on in any event. Sometimes, as described above in the 'cure' and 'Switzerland' scenarios, they are introduced by the patient anyway and my job is to go with them there and then.

Here is another example that sometimes crops up spontaneously:

P: I just don't know what to do… I feel like I've been through all this treatment and now I'm wasting the life I have…

Here, the implication is that they don't want to waste their life. But how to can you construct a solution-focused conversation around what the patient clearly wants to talk about? How do we get to know what an 'un-wasted' life might look like? If there is sense of mutual trust and safety, more often than not I will ask:

H: Right... so I guess you want to get it *right*. If I may ask you this question, suppose I could talk to you on the day you die, what would you *love* to be looking back on?

P: Well, I will have made sure the family's going to be OK [goes on to give a list, including security for the family plus small-but-meaningful experiences e.g., a walk through the woods and anything else they've never made time for before].

I would at that point seek to explore all of those things, but, for the sake of illustration, I will 'unpack' the first.

H: So... how will you know your family is well set up?

P: Well, they will have no money worries... things will be sorted like the money I've put aside for my funeral.

As you can see, through asking about the preferred future, instances of it already having happened emerge... a very common experience. Additionally, in my *opinion*[98], by 'going there' with the patient, I am, I hope, signalling that I *am* comfortable talking about death and other big questions. I feel this is important; being on a foreshortened life can be a lonely experience particularly if seemingly no-one amongst one's nearest-and-dearest can cope with talking about death. Also, it opens up opportunities to talk about fears about dying in pain, which can be addressed by my medical colleagues.

I remember asking the 'dying day' question to one guy and, quick as a flash, he came back with 'D'ya mean on my deathbed, what will I *not* be regretting?!'...which was close enough, certainly, to get a conversation going about what he *did* want!

---

[98] You may beg to differ...

Naturally, this approach of recruiting our end-goal to inform our present and near future is not original to me. One relatively recent example is the oft-repeated saying 'On their death-bed, no-one ever said I wish I'd spent more time at the office![99]'. It is also the underpinning of what in the UK are called 'Advance Care Plans[100]'.

Here's a lovely quote from Morrie Schwartz[101]:

> *"The best way to deal with that is to live in a fully conscious, compassionate, loving way. Don't wait until you're on your deathbed to recognize that this is the only way to live."*

Another way[102] of really getting down to what matters with patients within the Solution-Focused world, and potentially quite quickly, is the *Miracle Question[103]*.

> *"I am going to ask you a rather strange question [pause]. The strange question is this: [pause] After we talk, you will go back to your work (or home or school) and you will do whatever you need to do the rest of today, such as taking care of the children, cooking dinner, watching TV, giving the children a bath, and so on. It will be time to go to bed. Everybody in your household is quiet, and you are sleeping in peace. In the middle of the night, a miracle happens and the problem that prompted you to talk to me today is solved! But because this happens while you are sleeping, you have no way of knowing that there was an overnight miracle that solved the problem. [pause] So, when you wake up tomorrow morning, what might be the small change that will make you say to yourself, 'Wow, something must have happened—the problem is gone!'?"*

---

[99] Often attributed to Harold Kushner (1925-)

[100] For example, see https://www.nhs.uk/conditions/end-of-life-care/?tab name=planning-ahead accessed 10/06/2020

[101] That, and many more excellent deathbed quotes can be found at https://www.brainyquote.com/topics/deathbed-quotes (accessed 30/05/2020)

[102] I've included it for completeness in case the reader has heard of it elsewhere.

[103] Berg, I. K., & Dolan, Y. (2001). *Tales of solutions: A collection of hope-inspiring stories*. New York: Norton. p.7

I don't tend to use it in cancer settings as it *feels* like it probably belongs better in a different context[104]. Perhaps it is a little *too* nuclear, potentially insensitive, especially if the patient hadn't mentioned the word 'miracle' themselves. Instead, I have used a slightly 'lighter' version, asking people about what they would wish for.

I remember asking one 67-yer old gent in a hospice something along these lines[105]. I was asked to see him because he was deemed to have what is known as 'total pain'[106], a diagnosis which implies there is a strong psychological contribution to his pain because it had not been amenable to medication. Knowing that he was wary of people like me, my opening remark was "I'm the shrink you were warned about". This seemed to go down quite well, so I continued, asking if he had three wishes what he would hope for. One was seeing his

brother in Cornwall, another taking his wife to Scotland on a train for the scenery, but the one wish that most energised him was, of all things, *building a tepee for his granddaughter*[107]. He described at length what this would entail; procuring and utilising the particular

---

[104] My understanding is that one of the founders of the Solution-Focused approach, Insoo Kim Berg, invented it on the spot when a depressed man said to her something like *'It would take some kind of miracle for things to change…'*

[105] This is a good opportunity to plug 'something I made earlier'; a fuller version can be found in in Bray, D., Groves, K., Latham, J., Iddon, J. & Weymouth, E. (2015) ''First, do no harm': a solution-focused approach to pain measurement and management'. *European Journal of Palliative Care* **22**(4) 190-193.

[106] You may have guessed I think that diagnosis can have problems. If you're interested, see the 2015 paper referenced above.

[107] By the by, in a similar vein, I had the pleasure of meeting an entrepreneur farmer (also with advanced cancer) who had a talent for engineering and hearing about his plans for an industrial-sized carrot-sorting machine. You

marine plywood and varnish that would ultimately make this edifice bombproof. The implication being that the structure would be there long after him[108].

The 'moral of the story' is that there is a lot to be gained by beginning a discussion on a larger scale. A 'no-holds-barred' approach. "What is of ultimate importance right now, to you, however unusual and personalised it may be?"

This is quite different to a 'problem-solving' approach where a problem is identified and options generated from the present, debilitating situation.

In short, through the process of 'recruiting the future', SF 'starts from the other end', enabling people's wonderful creativity and resourcefulness to emerge; somehow it frees up the whole conversation to make a significant difference.

Yet another way of 'getting at' what really matters in a 'nuclear' way is asking "if this was your last day on earth… how would you know it had been well-spent?". This is, of course, very much the message of palliative care services: life *before* death; every life, however long or short, ***matters***.

In this sort of vein, I was once asked to see an older lady[109] (I'll call her Susan) in another hospice because of her anxiety and I was slightly at a loss as to how to go about it[110]. I decided to 'recruit the future' by asking her 'If I could come back tonight and you'd had a good day, what would you be pleased to be telling me?' Thankfully she 'got it' and straight away told me she wouldn't have too many

---

may have noticed *Huntapac* vegetables at Tesco's (other retail outlets are available)..

[108] Naturally I'm quoting this because it went well… his experience of pain was a lot better after our chat and stayed that way.

[109] Her terminology.

[110] Not unusual for me. In some ways, it is a good thing; sharing the patient's sense of 'disempowerment' helps me listen and therefore collaborate better. In SF literature, this is known and embraced as *the position of not-knowing*.

visitors and would be able to enjoy *Inspector Morse*[111]. As an obvious next step, I enquired how many was the *right number* of visitors. This turned out to be her husband and son only; she had lots of friends but they were too much. That was easily sorted with the nurses, who were asked to 'repel all boarders', which they were already well-versed in. Then I wondered about the TV show. It emerged that, being nearly blind, she got great pleasure from listening to the story, but couldn't have it loud enough to hear as the TV was too far away. Cue the extension lead...

In a similar vein, when walking through a ward for people with cancer, I happened upon this lady I'd met once before. This time it was dire; she had just slumped to the floor, having broken her hip through spread of cancer and I was first on the scene. She said 'I just want to die'. And she meant it. She knew her time was short anyway and she was being utterly rational, both she and I knew it. I had no idea what to do. Then it occurred to me; not only would it *not* be helpful to try and persuade her to live, but also, if she knew that wish were properly heard and respected, I may yet be of help, because she may yet want something. I sat down with her and said 'Right, Mary[112], yes... and would you like to stay here or shall I see if the nurses can help you back into bed?[113]' Mary chose the bed option; the implication being that, while she was waiting to die, she would prefer to be comfortable. And she did, just a few days later.

---

[111] For non-British readers, this was, and still is with its sequels, a stylish 2-hour detective show based on the books of Colin Dexter set in the dreaming spires of Oxford, originally starring the much-missed John Thaw (1942-2002).

[112] Made-up name.

[113] I hope if there are any nurses reading this thinking I'm stating the obvious and it's what they automatically do all the time, they will forgive me! The point here is how we as healthcare staff can reliably and consistently know what the right thing to do is by listening, and how to communicate to patients that we are listening, rather than assuming.

There was a lovely 'footnote' to Mary's story. The very same day as that horrible experience happened, the manicurist was on the ward. She had her nails done and *loved* it.

So, there's always a conversation to be had, a reason to inquire whether life is being lived well, however limiting the circumstances. Susan and Mary's stories illustrate another point; asking the right questions allows the smallest and yet most significant things of importance to emerge...

(ii) 'It may sound silly but...' Sometimes it's the little things that count most[114] (and some more ways to enable them to emerge)

P: I'm dreading Christmas...we're having my mother-in-law for dinner[115].

H: So, if we were to meet in early January, what would you *love* to be telling me about Christmas?

P: Hmmm... It may sound silly but... she always insists on fresh peas. It's a real nuisance shelling peas. I just get angrier every year and now I'm recovering from cancer, well... life's too short! So... for once... I would love to be serving frozen peas....

H: And what would *that* mean to you?

---

[114] Alexandra Adornetto (1994-)

[115] Yes, I did resist the obvious Les Dawson (1931-1993) comeback a la "what, all of her?". To cover myself, I will also note that he apparently also said "The mother-in-law is the centre of a family".

Sound far-fetched? It really happened![116] I've had all sorts of conversations over the years about peeling one's own potatoes, making one's own porridge, tying one's own shoelaces, etc. When people say some version of the 'silly, but...' statement, I know I've struck gold. Because however trivial they may assume it to be to others, it matters to *them*. It's a wonderful opportunity to affirm what they're saying and explore what those things represent; usually they have something to do with reclaiming control, agency and personhood.

Sometimes seemingly trivial things that really matter have to be achieved through influencing others. I would call this the 'chief executive' position; the way forward is for the 'ground floor' workers do the 'hands-on' work, but the inspiration lies elsewhere. In this respect, the laundry is a classic example:

P: He never hangs out the sheets properly!

S[117]: They get dry, don't they?

P: Yes, but you don't do them like I do so they aren't as good!

S: But does it really matter?

---

[116] And yes, she did...

[117] Spouse or other household member.

P: Well it matters to me![118]

Similar conversations also regularly occur about the garden, sundry housework, washing the car, etc.

So, as well as the using 'nuclear' questions mentioned before, what steers the conversation (so we really get to the point) as with the examples above? What else enables what *really matters* to emerge?

Here are some useful questions that crop up in appointments; you might like to try them for yourself in the context you're in right now, starting with some that apply when someone's significantly struggling:

- What does a good day look like for you?
- Failing that: What does an average day look like for you (as opposed to an averagely bad one)?
- Failing that: What does a bad day look like for you (as opposed to the worst[119])?

The point here is that, by really listening and noticing the difference between a 'really bad' and an 'averagely bad' day, we establish what 'less bad' looks like, which is a probably a small bit of what 'good' might look like. Here are some more examples, which fit better when the person is not quite so low as those who need the 'bad/really bad' questions:

- Suppose this conversation today was[120] really useful. Who would be the *first* to notice?

---

[118] There then follows some to-ing and fro-ing where the significance hopefully becomes apparent and is embraced...

[119] You might think I've suddenly gone all negative here. The reason for this is that this has worked better with people with intractable conditions like long-term pain; ask them about a good day and a significant proportion will say (or at least think) "What??! I never have a good day!"

[120] I realise that grammatically it should be something like *'were to be'* really useful, but, in conversation, the chief aim is to enable change to happen with normal language, not to be academically perfect.

- If I were a fly on the wall at your home, what would I see you doing later today?
- Supposing Millie were a particularly perceptive dog, what would she be telling me was different?
- If you and I were, sat down again in, say, four weeks' time, what would you *love* to be telling me?

As regards the 'Millie' question, you might be surprised by the great answers dog-owners have come up with. They include:

- I would be taking her out more.
- I would spend more time in the garden; she loves to have me watch her run around.
- I would throw the ball in my living room nine times rather than just twice.

And, of course, the same ideas apply to alternative significant others, most notably grandchildren, although they may be less inclined to play 'fetch' and more interested in being read a story. For example:

- What would you love[121] Daisy-Mae to be noticing about you after today's appointment?

---

[121] You may have noticed the language of the heart quote often. This tends to be what happens when the conversation is about what really *matters*. This is 'meaning of life' stuff (or as professionals call it 'spiritual goals').

I prescribe a bed-time story for Daisy-Mae.
Yes, 'The Tiger who Came to Tea', at least three times a week!

And then, as with all these questions, there's a follow-up, and a follow-up to the follow-up. Here's an example:

H: So, if she noticed you, as you say, being more 'fun' grandad and cracking silly jokes, what would that mean to her?

P: She'd be 'made up'[122]. Her little face would light up and she'd tell me to 'stop being a silly grumps'!

H: And if her face lit up and she told you off like that, what would that mean to you?

P: I'd be made up. Feel more like me again, like there was still something to look forward to!

So… as you read, should you wish to, you can substitute 'reading this book' (below) for appointment… and see what answers you might come up with. For example:

---

[122] A common expression in Merseyside where I work, meaning something like 'thoroughly glad'.

H: Who'd be the very first to notice that reading this book had made a difference?

P[123]: My [*insert name of your significant other*]. I'd stop being a pain. I'd... be a bit more like me again!'

H: What would that mean to them?

P: They'd be much happier; we'd laugh out loud again.

H: What difference would that make to you?

P: I'd feel more *hope*. Even if just for a short while.

H: How would [significant other] know you were feeling more hope?

P: I'd be agreeing to do things again...

H: What s-

P: [interrupting] In fact I would be suggesting things, planning things like I used to!

H: What's the smallest thing [significant other] might notice to tell them that was happening again?

P: I'd be suggesting we went out tomorrow to our favourite, feel-good place!

H: And what difference would that make to them?

P: They'd be so relieved... like I'd turned a corner!

H: And what difference would that make to you?

P: I would feel that too....

An alternative version:

---

[123] In this case, you!

H: How would you know the money you've shelled out on this book was well spent?

P[124]: I wouldn't feel like I've wasted it on yet another self-help book that's a flash-in-the-pan, feel-good-now, feel-just-the-same-tomorrow experience....

H: Ah... so at what point *would* you really know it had been worth your heard-earned money?

P: Hmmm... say in a week.

H: So... what *would* you be really pleased to be noticing next weekend...?

P: Hmmm... Hmmm... I wouldn't feel like I've wasted some more of my life by staying in bed most of the day....

H: Hmmm... so you're hoping for something a bit better than that?

P: Yes... something to get up for.

H: So... the money for this book will have been well spent if you find that you are getting up, perhaps shall we say a bit earlier than you would have done, maybe because you've got up for something?

P: ... yes....

H: ... and what times in your life *have you* found something worth getting up for?

P: xxxxxxxx[125]

(iii) Even more questions that can unlock your preferred future

As you did previously, you can, in the (relevant) questions below, substitute 'reading this book' for 'appointment' (or vice-versa):

---

[124] Still you!
[125] Censored as there's a lot more of that in Chapter 4....

- How come, given current difficulties, you turned up for your appointment?
- How will you know it's been worth two bus rides/the parking charges/getting childcare etc…?
- How will your referrer know they didn't make a dreadful mistake by referring you to me?
- You've stayed in for this phone-call/video appointment… what have you missed? How good will this have to be to make up for that?
- What made you buy/borrow this book in the first place?
- So… you came to the appointment under duress! What would this person twisting your arm be pleased to see so they would get off your back?
- So… you wanted to be here, but it's not about you, you don't mind what happens to you…it's about your family. What do you mind happens to them? How will you know you've done everything you possibly can for them?
- If you could go back in time, what would be better?
- If you had a hundred million pounds…[126]

Sometimes what people want are practical things…

hmmmm…tough choice….

---

[126] Or the currency of your choice.

…in which case, do ask about who and what is out there; Macmillan, Citizens' Advice Bureaux, cancer charities etc.

What do you *really, really, want?*

So, as you come to the end of this chapter, let's take a moment.

Have you ever been 'yes, butted' in appointments? Or in general life? If so, and if instead you'd heard 'yes… and', what would you have said?

If you were sat it an appointment with an at least half-competent Solution-Focused helper, which of the questions in this chapter would have got you interested? If none, what question(s) would you wish they'd asked you… and what would your response have been?

In all cases, were you to be given a chance, by someone else, to talk about what really matters, how would you like them to respond to your dreams? And, if they did respond that way, what difference would it make to you? How would they know they'd got it right? How would your significant other(s) know they'd got it right too?

What would your very own 'it may sound, silly but…' statements be?

Post-script to Chapter 3

"If you don't know where the hole is, it's a long day on the golf-course[127]". A little time invested in working out where you really, really want to go saves a lot of time going elsewhere.

---

[127] Michael F. Hoyt (1996) *A Golfer's Guide to Brief Therapy (With Footnotes for Baseball Fans)*, in *Constructive Therapies 2*. Guildford Press: NY.

CHAPTER FOUR[128]

RECRUITING WHAT YOU ALREADY KNOW

"He has half the deed done who has made a beginning"[129]

> **Chapter summary:**
> - **Powerful questions that make new lives possible;**
> - **Examples of the emergence of 'made-to-measure' new lives, for the next five minutes or fifty years;**
> - **Some more long words and another poem.**

The story so far…

We've invested time in listening. There's been ample opportunity, I hope, in Chapters 1 and 2 for proper listening in respect of how hard cancer, at whatever stage, can be. Then I went on about another kind of listening in Chapter 3—of what's in your heart and what *really matters* when the chips are down, just like what might happen in a good, solution-focused, appointment. But there's yet more listening to be done: *what do you already know about being the very best version of you?*

The usual 'medical model[130]' rests on the pillars of 'history' and the observed signs and self-reported symptoms. The SF model uses a quite different 'lens'; it looks at the same information from an *asset*,

---

[128] You may notice the chapters getting shorter. This isn't because I've run out of ideas. It's a reflection of what happens in a conversation; once the patient feels listened to and they have a sense of a future, things speed up!

[129] Horace (BC 65-08)

[130] Also known as the 'illness', or 'pathological', model. This is not, by the way, to suggest all medics practice exclusively in that fashion.

rather than a *deficit*, point of view. In short, it is much more interested in what's right, rather than what's wrong.

It's true that there are indeed deficits as well as assets. It just seems to turn out better when the focus is on assets[131]. So, the SF model is very much about partnership:

Like the letters through a stick of rock:

The SF model – less of:

---

[131] For the enthusiast, there's much more about all this stuff in Chapter 7!

The SF model – more of:

*...if the pot of gold at the end of the rainbow is where you want to be, the 'medical' black bag represents the strengths **you** already have in getting there.*

(i) A particular kind of 'history taking'

Perhaps we could take up from where we left off in Chapter 3.

H: So... the money for this book will have been well spent if you find that you are getting up, perhaps shall we say a bit earlier than you would have done, maybe because you've got up for something...?

P: Yes...

H.... and what times in your life have you found something worth getting up for?

P: .... hmmmmm... I used to like to go out first thing in the morning for my paper... it was all quiet then... no-one to bother me....

H: ... so what was that like?

P: ... peace... like I was free to be myself....

H: ... is that still important to you?

P: … yes, it is; more so now.

H: … so there have been times in your life when that's happened before?

P: … yes… like when I'm reading a really good novel and I get lost in it and no-one bothers me…

H: [noticing change of tense] So what are you reading now?

P: A strange one for me… it's one I spotted on my favourite internet site that suggests good reads. This one's about a detective in the time of Henry VIII. Getting really interesting hearing about how Tudor people had a lot of the same problems we did[132].

As *you* read this, and hopefully by applying the principle of *listen hard… and when it's really bad, listen harder*, you may have noticed for yourself the person's use of 'my'. This shows that the person was willing to give something new a try, and is persisting, that they have an enquiring mind, that the person gets comfort from others being in a similar position, and even that the person is getting energised…

This is a very common experience in SF appointments.

When *what matters* has been firmly established, instances of it actually happening tend to emerge. The trick is to listen. So, dear reader…

- What *matters* to you? What do you *hope* for?
- What do you already know about being that person, and know about getting there? What times historically, presently, or even potentially in the future, can you recall or foresee you being that person, or those things happening?

---

[132] If you're interested, I'm referring to the *Shardlake* series by C.J. Sansom. A great read!

From trauma, comes healing...

Here's another example drawn from my experiences[133] as a clinical psychologist. A few years back, I was asked to see a woman inpatient in her late 30s. It turned out she was a nurse in the same hospital and had undergone surgery for breast cancer, but had largely withdrawn, literally facing the wall, to the added consternation of her colleagues.

I can't quite remember the exact course of the conversation, but I eventually gleaned she literally didn't want to face this new life. It was overwhelming, impossibly scary; she couldn't imagine how she could ever get on with her life knowing that *it could happen to me*. And yet... she was a committed wife, a mother to two young-ish children and a nurse who loved her job, who, herself, *made a difference.*

I was, as so often happens, at a loss. After all, she was being entirely rational; it had happened to her and no-one could truthfully say it could never happen again (does this sound familiar to you as you read this now?).

The best course of action I could think of was to keep the conversation going until something came up; to do that *'listen harder'* thing I talked of in Chapter 3.

And, as so often happens, it did. I asked her something along the lines of:

'Have you ever had to deal with stuff happening before?'

It had. A good few months back, she'd been driving along without a care in the world when *quite without warning* a red car had emerged from a side road and went straight into the side of her, which wrote off her car. Cue questions:

- *What was that like?*

---

[133] I'm aware this could all sound a bit smug as I talk about things that have gone well! I mention real-life stories to bring the book to life.

- *I've noticed you've been working until very recently, but you live a distance away—does that mean you're driving again?*
- *Yes? Hmm… given how shaken up you were for quite a while after, how on earth did you ever get driving again? What did that take?*
- *Through that experience what did you learn about yourself?*

Who would have known that a car crash would turn out to be a good thing? A classic 'blessing in disguise?' And yet it was.

Through re-visiting, not so much the incident itself, but what it took to get driving again (one bit at a time as she told me) and what that implied about her (someone who can be traumatised and have a first-hand experience that not only can 'stuff happen', but, most importantly, that one can learn to live with the knowledge that it can happen again), she began to believe in herself and the future again. Oh, and apparently the other thing that helped was me not wearing a tie.[134]

Have you had any 'car crash' experiences in your life that might yet help you to deal with the present and future?

This is why a good conversation, with a helpful person, can make a difference; not only may they see things you don't, but also you may realise these things for yourself through explaining yourself out loud[135].

(ii) A particular kind of observation: noticing 'keeping going-ness[136]'

On another occasion, and in a different hospital, I was asked to see an elderly lady with advanced cancer who would only ever talk to

---

[134] Perhaps it signalled to her I wasn't going to be 'an expert' telling her what to do.

[135] Obviously, this is not a remotely original observation on my part.

[136] Winston Churchill himself apparently said *"When you're going through hell, keep going!"*

staff about 'white spots[137]', not cancer, and how she had these great plans for when she got out of hospital. To compound everyone else's worry, she would not talk frankly with her grown-up son. A succession of colleagues had had a go at inviting her into a frank conversation, but it wasn't happening. Was she in *denial*? Cue referral to psychologist...

Where do you begin a conversation like that? In truth, I hadn't a clue, other than promising myself I would consciously *not* try to jolly her out of her apparently unwise stance.[138]

So... back to basic principles; keep the conversation going long enough, show proper respect and something good may happen.

I sat on her bed[139] and just had a chat... 'how's it going for you?' and all that.

Then I was saved by the arrival of the W.R.V.S.[140] lady with her trolley of sweets and newspapers!

The 'lady with white spots' politely interrupted me and said something like

'Excuse me for a moment... I like to get the paper[141]'

---

[137] I only found out afterwards that she was referring to white spots on X-Rays she'd obviously been shown. The fact that I didn't even know that, and, as it turned out, didn't need to know that, is a further example of the solution-focused principle of 'not-knowing', i.e., in this case the patient was the expert. Somewhere, vaguely, I had some awareness that cancer can look like that on an X-Ray but she knew a lot more than me!

[138] For example, saying 'you do realise you have cancer, don't you?'... accompanied by a winning smile.

[139] I didn't know better in those days...

[140] The Women's Royal Voluntary Service, known as the Royal Voluntary Service since 2013. They do excellent work, amongst other things in UK hospitals running shops.

[141] It was the *Daily Express*, by the way. I'm not sure what this particular choice could have told me at the time...

Then it came to me. The clue was in the present tense of the 'like'. The implication was... *this is something she does regularly in hospital.* So, my next question was:

'Hmmm... what else do you do in here that works for you?'

I can't even remember what she said next. What I can remember is a short while after me saying:

'Sounds like you know what you're doing. So, you must have a good reason for talking about "white spots" and the plans you have after hospital.'

Sure enough, she did. And she was gracious enough to share them with me. The gist was that, some weeks ago, after the news was broken to her, she had met with a very good friend and they'd had a good cry together, and as she saw it, being pessimistic and miserable would not be *her*. Her tone, in the nicest possible way, was along the lines of 'don't worry young man, I know what I'm doing...!'

It was quite natural to follow up with:

'So, I guess you have reasons for not discussing this with your son?'

And, indeed, she did. They were very close, him never having married and being an only child. She knew that if they did have that frank conversation, he would rely on her to prop him up. At this stage, she felt the most loving thing to do was to teach him to stand on his own two feet. She knew he would have to, sooner rather than later. She knew full-well that her time could well be short.

So... my starting point is always to assume people have good reason for handling things the way they do until proved otherwise[142]. That way, you'll listen better.

Dear reader... have you been misunderstood, judged even for the way you handle things? What *good reason(s)* could you enlighten

---

[142] Hardly an original thought! See also 'Confessions of a Pharmacist' later in this book.

someone else with, were they to properly look and listen? What 'expertise-in-disguise' do *you* have?

Here's another way of uncovering strengths, expertise and assets. You might remember this graph from Chapter 1[143]:

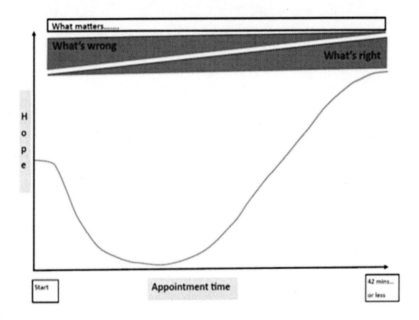

This is what you might well experience if this was a SF appointment. As you begin the conversation and take a step back from the day-to-day and contemplate your life with cancer, [144] it's common to experience an initial 'sinking of the spirits'. We tend to go straight to the negatives, which does not mean we are doing that on purpose for attention or to manipulate the conversation.

---

[143] Unless, of course, you skipped straight to Chapter 3, in which case repeating it here will save you the bother!

[144] Again, I'm implying here that even after an 'all-clear', one can never *not* have had cancer once one has had it…for more on this, see Chapter 5.

So here we are at the bottom of the curve. John Bunyan might have called this the *Slough of Despond*.[145] Strangely enough, this can be a great 'place' to uncover strengths. You might find these sorts of questions useful as you read this book, just as they frequently are in an appointment:

- What *does it take* to keep going?
- What *does it take* to get through the day?
- What gets you out of bed *at all*?
- How come you haven't given up?
- How come you're still seeking help by attending this appointment [reading this book]? What does it take to keep hoping like that?
- What are you doing that is stopping things being even worse?
- What have you learned from previous hard times that's helping you now?
- Did you *even know* you could do this?
- Who would be *least* surprised you're keeping going[146]?
- What are your nearest and dearest learning from *you*?
- Etc.

Hopefully, the respectful 'both/and' mentality, where both the difficulty and the effort are affirmed, is clear. And, as I mentioned earlier, I'm writing this book in the midst of the COVID-19 crisis and these questions have, in a sense, been the 'only show in town'. The only ones that are both respectful of how darned difficult it is to get through Lockdown and, at the same time, lead anywhere therapeutic, in the sense of leading to a feeling of hope, which is what it's all about.

---

[145] The Pilgrim's Progress by John Bunyan, 1678. But without any implication that state of mind is a result of self-inflicted wounds; more as a reaction to circumstances.

[146] I call this the 'Aunty Vera' question as so many people in Merseyside, where I do a lot of my work, seem to have one, who, furthermore, would be able to identify some key qualities in them.

(iii) A particular kind of observation: noticing 'the problem *not* happening'

In short, standard medical practice pays attention to the hole. In contrast, SF practice gets interested in the doughnut[147]. Problems almost always have exceptions; that is, times when they're absent, less frequent or less intense… and, by implication, there is a *presence* of something better. In these cases, there is a 'doughnut', however wafer thin it may begin to appear

This is not inconsequential detail. This can completely turn around the way someone looks at their life, helping them start to live it better. In the context we're talking about, frequently this will mean times when people don't actually think about cancer all the time, even though they had been convinced such thoughts were always there.

And here is the 'plot spoiler'. The answer more often than not is grand-children or dogs[148], as we illustrated in Chapter 3.

Here's how conversations tend to play out[149]:

H: How's life at the moment?

P: It's really hard. I can't stop thinking about cancer all the time. I think I'm going mad. It's doing my head in…

H: Sounds like hard work…

P: Yes, it's there all the time.

H: Hmmm… what gets you through the day?

---

[147] I think this metaphor was created by Bill O'Hanlon (1952-)

[148] Other pets are available! But dogs seem to 'tick most of the boxes', especially going out.

[149] I've used 'cancer worry' as an example as it's very common, but these questions can be applied to many problems, not just psychological ones.

P: I don't... I just *exist.*[150]

H: Blimey.... What does it take even to *exist*?

P: Everything I've got...

H: And why do you do it?

P: Well, you have to, don't you?

H: Do you? What's telling you that you have to keep doing it?

P: Well, it's the family... you've got to for them...

H: Oh... so who's in your family?

P: Well, I divorced years ago, but I still see a lot of my grandchildren.

H: How many have you got?

P: Just Amy and Sam. I have Amy on a Wednesday.

H: And what do you do on a Wednesday?

P: When the weather's good, we go to the park. If it's bad, we stay in and I play with her at home.

H: And when you're at the park, what do you notice about yourself?

P: We just play. Sometimes I even get on the swings myself!

H: So, what are you thinking about when you do that?

P: Nothing really, she's my whole world [smiles]!

H: Same when you're playing at home with her?

P: Yes... I make up silly voices and she giggles [beams].

---

[150] You may have noticed this patient is intent on telling me how rubbish it is and doesn't make it easy for me. This happens!

H: So… you'd like 'more of that please'… those 'Amy moments' when she's your whole world and cancer really doesn't get much of a look in?

P: That's it… [appointment continues].

You could substitute a dog's name above and have much the same conversation.

So, dear reader, what and when are your 'Amy moments'?

> *Perhaps when you're in the garden, walking through the woods, reading a good book, cleaning the car, or cross-stitching, etc.?*

The same principle applies to pain. Pain, like thinking about cancer, is of course compelling and tends to 'build up its part', growing in importance in our thinking, as our belief in its power and its presence grows.

Here's another list of useful questions, this time on the 'exceptions' theme[151]:

- What were *you* doing last Wednesday? On reflection, did you think about your worries all day long?

---

[151] If you find in reading these that you're thinking 'he doesn't know how tough it is, he's taking the Michael', you may wish to (re)visit Chapters 1 and 2.

- What are the signs of you not worrying (or at least not worrying at the worst level it can be for you)? When did they last happen?
- When did you last start to worry but something else came along that took your mind off it?
- If you were to 'coach' someone else like you who wants to worry less, what would you tell them *not* to do, where would you tell them *not* to go, and, given all that, what /where would you suggest they did/went instead?
- How come you're not completely off your head with worry; how come you're still sane at all?
- How is it that you're even slightly able to concentrate on hearing me right now [reading this book]?

Questions that work well when there is already some 'light at the end of the tunnel' include:

- What are you good at?
- What do you do with your life (when not stuck at home)?
- What do you already know about [for example, relaxation]?
- What's worked before?
- What *did* it take to get to this appointment [read so far in this book]?
- What is better on a slightly less bad day?
- What strengths are you known for?
- What does your manager have to say about your qualities in your annual appraisal?
- What qualities would your spouse/friend/family member/dog say you had?

And similar questions work well when we look at the family as an entity:

- What strengths do you have or are known for as a family?
- How have you got through things in the past as a family? (NB: This is not the same as 'what have you got through in the past?')

Family and friends can also be 'recruited' as 'noticers' in a very helpful way. As well as significant others, one can involve even young children in noticing, and therefore reinforcing, strengths. For example:

- Daisy, I'd like you to catch your Nan out! Without telling her, please spot Nan being 'fun Nan' and 'tell' on her to me!

More ways to uncover strengths: making numbers count

More often than not, in healthcare settings, 10 (on a scale of 10) is where you don't want to be, such as when pain is being assessed. SF looks at things the other way around:

- Suppose 10, on a scale of 10, is you living life to the full, and 0 is none of that happening, where are you between 0 and 10?
- What makes it that number[152] (and not lower)?
- What else makes it that number?
- How are you even doing those things?
- How did you even get there?
- What does all that say about you?

Your life on a scale:

---

[152] A remarkable number of patients say 'er, two or three' when I first meet them.

...if the pot of gold at the end of the rainbow is where you want to be, the black bag represents the strengths you already have in getting there, arriving further up the scale.

You may well ask 'what if I'm at '0'?'

Then I'd be inviting you to think about:

- How on earth *am* I keeping going?
- What does *that* take?
- What does that say about me?

Concluding thoughts: The power of noticing and a mission

Whether through being asked about a history of strengths, or invited to pay attention to present ones, the message is the same. That is:

Yes, there has been a lot of hard stuff in your life, hard stuff now and most likely into the future. And it's also true that you are still standing. This says something about you that it's profoundly helpful to recognise and build on. The better you get at recognising these strengths and capitalising on them[153], the quicker you will get to the life that really matters to you.

---

[153] In psychology circles, this is known as positive selective abstraction. More of this in Chapter 6.

As you read, this is your mission, should you choose to accept it[154].

---

[154] *Mission: Impossible.* CBS Television 1966 onward.

CHAPTER FIVE

NEXT STEPS IN THIS ALTERNATIVE LIFE: "HOW DO YOU EAT AN ELEPHANT?"[155]

"Medicine cannot heal in a vacuum; it requires connection"[156]

Chapter summary:

- Powerful questions and examples that bring new lives within reach;
- Some thoughts on finding 'contentment';
- Some more long words and two stories;
- Walking 'in step' with health professionals.

Pretty much without exception.

The people I see never resume the old 'normal' again. They can never *not have had* cancer. But here's the good news. The new normal is often a better version of themselves. There is a better perspective; what matters, and what doesn't. There is a better appreciation for the richness of life: 'life in high definition', if you will. Like the joy of grandchildren or dogs.

You may wish to look up 'Post-Traumatic Growth' (the theory that explains transformation following trauma). And having that residual

---

[155] Often attributed to Confucius (BC 551-479). The punchline, depending on which version you've heard, is 'one small piece at a time'.

[156] Rana Awdish (2018) *In Shock: how nearly dying made me a better intensive care doctor.* Fabulous book.

anxiety, that sense of 'yes it can happen to me', actually spurs people on. Life's not forever. Now where do I go from here?

Taking that first step…

He has the deed half done who has made a beginning[157].

Being daunted by the task ahead seems to happen a lot and, given the age of the quote and many like it since, it always did. Doesn't everything feel like a mountain, when to others it looks like a molehill? Isn't it easy to feel defeated by what's ahead before we even start? So, the only logical thing is to make a small start. As Jon Bon Jovi put it, on the character's way to 'Saturday night'[158]:

> *Hey man I'm alive I'm takin' each day a night at a time*
> *Yeah I'm down but I know I'll get by*
> *Hey, hey, hey, hey man I've gotta live my life*
> *I'm gonna pick up all the pieces of what's left of my pride*
> *I'm feelin' like a Monday but someday I'll be Saturday night*

…by making numbers count, again

In Chapter 4, we thought about where you might be up to on a scale of 10, in terms of the life you'd really want.

Let's suppose you said '3'. At that point, I would invite you to think of every possibly way in which your life is a '3' and not lower, and what this says about you. Now we can take this a step further:

- How will you know when you're at a '4'?

If I may interrupt the flow here, the question is *not:*

- What do you have to do to get from '3' to a '4'?

That would belong to a classical 'problem solving' approach, which invites respondents to generate a list of possible options and choose

---

[157] Horace (65-8 BC)
[158] From the album *Cross Road* (1994) Mercury.

one. From experience, when I've heard that question asked by others, it's met with, at best, 'don't know' and, at worst, 'If I knew that I wouldn't be here talking to you [or in this case, reading the book]!' Asking the question, SF-style, from the point of view of the *step already having happened* is quite a different thing.

It's bringing that 'preferred future' (i.e., *what really matters*) within touching distance and it allows multiple levels of experience, and others' perspectives, to be 'recruited' to give life and substance to the hope:

- How will you know when you're at a '4'?
- What will that feel like?
- What difference will that make to you?
- How will others (such as your spouse, your children, or your dog) know that you're at a '4'?
- What's the very first thing they might notice?
- What difference will that make to them?

Sometimes, moving one whole point of a scale of 10 is too big a step. This would be particularly true if your initial point was '0'. So, the preferred future can be brought even closer[159] to where you already are:

- You're at a '0' and we've talked about *just what it takes even to keep going*[160]. You've said you would like to get off 'rock bottom', but it's quite overwhelming. How would you know you'd even got as far as 0.1?
- What would that mean to you?
- Etc.

---

[159] This is known as 'salami-slicing', origin unknown.
[160] Covered in Chapter 4

There's an inspirational story[161] about a man who set out to re-forest a desolate valley, one acorn at a time:

In 1910, while hiking through the wild lavender in a wind-swept, desolate valley in Provence, a man came across a shepherd who would sort, and then plant, hundreds of acorns, one by one, as he walked through the wilderness.

Ten years later, after surviving the First World War, the man re-visits the shepherd and sees the young forest he has created spreading slowly over the valley. The narrator returns year after year to see the miracle the shepherd is gradually creating: a verdant, green landscape that is a testament to one man's creative instinct

...even more on making numbers count...

Questions about one's level of confidence,[162] in even the smallest amount of change happening, can be a rewarding way of uncovering *even more* strengths. They go something like this:

- **H:** So... you're already at a two because these [examples] are happening. On a scale of ten, ten being totally confident, how confident are you that things will get to, say, a two-and-a-half?

- **P:** Hmmmm... say five or six.

- **H:** Right... what makes it *five or six* and not lower?

- **P:** Er…. well … ummm... well I've had to cope with difficult things in life before.

---

[161] Jean Giono (1954) *The Man who Planted Trees*. Harvill Press: London (abridged).

[162] This is a good place to acknowledge my debt to The Brief Group www.brief.org.uk (accessed 10/06/2022), who first showed me the power of confidence questions and many other things. Going on one of their four-day training courses in SF in 1996 changed my career.

- **H:** Ah… right… what did it take to cope with difficult things before?

- **P:** Hmmm… just keeping going. One day at a time….

- **H:** And what would get you through *those* days?

- **P:** Doing what I needed to do, just focusing on those things and not looking too far ahead.

- **H:** Right… and *what else* gives you five or six confidence that things will get better, even a bit?

- **P:** Hmmm… my old mum[163] [164]used to say I could do anything if I set my mind to it!

- **H:** Aha… did she say that to everyone or did she particularly say that to you?

- **P:** Ah… well… I was hard work for her because I always wanted to do things for myself… and usually did… so I was known as 'the wild child' when she was being polite.

- **H:** And when she wasn't…?

- **P:** …I'd better not say!

- **H:** So what qualities, if she were here, would she say you have?

- **P:** Determination, keeping at something I believe in… don't give up…

---

[163] In different places, people would express this differently. Here in the Northwest of England, people would often say 'Me Ma…'
[164] It's a particular pleasure in Merseyside to uncover stories of generations of strong women who go on to inspire the next.

- **H:** And how would she know you were just the same in dealing with things now?

- **P:** I'd be [lists off small but significant things that matter].

- **H:** Right! And what else is telling you, you *might just get there…*?

As you can see from the above example[165], inviting someone to view themselves, *as if through someone else's eyes,* particularly when they spontaneously mention them, can be a powerful way of bringing a sense of confidence and well-founded hope into a conversation.

How to **want** *to take that first step: finding 'contentment' in this new life…*

Around two thousand years ago, a political prisoner wrote that he had 'learned to be content in all circumstances'[166]. So far in this chapter, I've shared some things I do in appointments that help people move on from where they are, even if only a little bit. But supposing that rankles? Suppose, as can happen in an appointment, the idea of choosing to embrace this new life, however tentatively, is a bitter pill, a disappointment, even a significant loss?

Well, just as within an appointment I might re-visit how normal those feelings and associated experiences are, you may wish to re-visit Chapters 1 and 2.

But there is one more thing that you might wish to try; to explore whether it might just be possible in your circumstances to find at least *contentment*, and not just dull surrender. Once again, a good story, in the form of a modern parable[167] might be helpful. Although it is

---

[165] And in Chapter 4 with the 'Aunty Vera' question.

[166] Paul of Tarsus writing in Philippians 4:11-14, paraphrased.

[167] Kingsley, E.P. (1987, accessed 10/06/2022) Welcome to Holland https://www.emilyperlkingsley.com/welcome-to-holland

written for a particular context, many have found it helpful over the years, including myself.

'Welcome to Holland'

Emily Perl Kingsley

I am often asked to describe the experience of raising a child with a disability—to try to help people who have not shared that unique experience to understand it, to imagine how it would feel. It's like this…

When you're going to have a baby, it's like planning a fabulous vacation trip to Italy. You buy a bunch of guide books and make your wonderful plans. The Coliseum. The Michelangelo David. The gondolas in Venice. You may learn some handy phrases in Italian. It's all very exciting.

After months of eager anticipation, the day finally arrives. You pack your bags and off you go. Several hours later, the plane lands. The stewardess comes in and says, "Welcome to Holland."

"Holland?!?" you say. "What do you mean Holland?? I signed up for Italy! I'm supposed to be in Italy. All my life I've dreamed of going to Italy."

But there's been a change in the flight plan. They've landed in Holland and there you must stay.

The important thing is that they haven't taken you to a horrible, disgusting, filthy place, full of pestilence, famine and disease. It's just a different place.

So you must go out and buy new guide books. And you must learn a whole new language. And you will meet a whole new group of people you would never have met.

It's just a different place. It's slower-paced than Italy, less flashy than Italy. But after you've been there for a while and you catch your breath, you look around... and you begin to notice that Holland has windmills... and Holland has tulips. Holland even has Rembrandts.

But everyone you know is busy coming and going from Italy... and they're all bragging about what a wonderful time they had there. And for the rest of your life, you will say "Yes, that's where I was supposed to go. That's what I had planned."

And the pain of that will never, ever, ever, ever go away... because the loss of that dream is a very, very significant loss.

But... if you spend your life mourning the fact that you didn't get to Italy, you may never be free to enjoy the very special, the very lovely things ... about Holland.

I think the parable speaks loudly of any situation where someone is being invited to embrace the life they have rather than the one they had in mind. This is clearly a deeply personal choice[168]. In reading this book, just as I might put it to you in an appointment, I would invite you to think about, once again:

What do you really, really want?

Is it better to be stuck in a half-life of 'if only' or is it better to try, bit-by-bit, to make a go of it? For example, are you better off staying at home because you can't bring yourself to use a wheelchair... or would it be worth a go? If it's the stay-at-home option for you, may I refer you to a question I introduced earlier[169]:

H: Suppose I could talk to you on the day you die, what would you *love* to be looking back on?

---

[168] Although I would say it's always important to be mindful of the consequences of our choices on our 'nearest and dearest' to be fair to them too.

[169] Chapter 3.

Growth in adversity: your continued mission to notice 'blessings in disguise'

There is more. As it turns out, and as hinted at in 'Welcome to Holland', there may yet turn out to be something(s) unexpected or life-affirming, something(s) you would never have had without this major change in your life plans. Some 'blessings in disguise' even?

This is variously known as *Post-Traumatic Growth* or *Flourishing*. As I mentioned before, I call it *Life in High Definition*[170], in which, yes, the trees really are more beautiful, relationships matter more and material things generally less, unless it's in the context of taking care of loved-ones' future[171].

From my experience in appointments, this seems to be the 'upside' to the Damocles Syndrome[172][173]. As people become aware that life is finite, they experience the joy of being alive more intensely, in some cases for the very first time. It's that thing about human beings needing contrast. As ex-President Nixon put it:

> *"Only if you have been in the deepest valley, can you ever know how magnificent it is to be on the highest mountain."*[174]

---

[170] I expect that someone else has made that comparison too…

[171] If you're reading this and at the point of throwing the book out the window, thinking 'he's minimising my suffering, what does he know', you may wish to re-read Chapters 1 and 2.

[172] Chapter 2.

[173] I'm aware that philosophers and suchlike will have made the same point since time immemorial.

[174] https://www.brainyquote.com/quotes/richard_m_nixon_159252 accessed 10/06/2022.

New life from unpromising beginnings*:*

As you read this, just as you might be in an appointment, would you be interested in answering these questions:

- *What's different, but somehow better now?*
- *What 'blessings in disguise' have you noticed?*
- *What really matters now?*
- *Are you making different choices, such as being less busy at work?*
- *Are you making more effort with relationships and are they deeper?*
- *What matters less?*
- *What are you already doing to use your time well with the right people doing the right things?*
- **Are you consciously *living well*?**

And here's another inspirational story; this one's about starfish[175], and it encompasses both the idea of one-bit-at-a-time and affirming life even in the midst of loss:

---

[175] The original story is by Loren Eiseley (1907–1977) in *The Star Thrower*, pub. 1978, Random House: New York, but it has many versions. This one is by Peter Straube, https://eventsforchange.wordpress.com/2011/06/05/the-starfish-story-one-step-towards-changing-the-world/ (accessed 10/06/2022).

'The Star Thrower'

Once upon a time, there was an old man who used to go to the ocean to do his writing. He had a habit of walking on the beach every morning before he began his work. Early one morning, he was walking along the shore after a big storm had passed and found the vast beach littered with starfish as far as the eye could see, stretching in both directions.

Off in the distance, the old man noticed a small boy approaching. As the boy walked, he paused every so often and as he grew closer, the man could see that he was occasionally bending down to pick up an object and throw it into the sea. The boy came closer still and the man called out, "Good morning! May I ask what it is that you are doing?"

The young boy paused, looked up, and replied "Throwing starfish into the ocean. The tide has washed them up onto the beach and they can't return to the sea by themselves," the youth replied. "When the sun gets high, they will die, unless I throw them back into the water."

The old man replied, "But there must be tens of thousands of starfish on this beach. I'm afraid you won't really be able to make much of a difference."

The boy bent down, picked up yet another starfish and threw it as far as he could into the ocean. Then he turned, smiled and said, "It made a difference to that one!"

Two steps forward…

At the risk of stating the obvious once again, it's entirely *usual* for there to be setbacks:

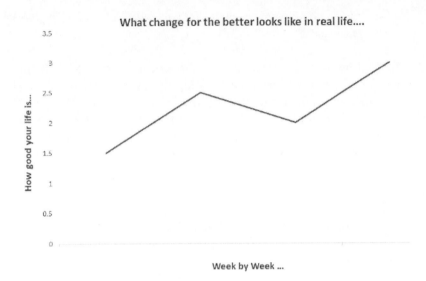

So, it will be a case of 'two steps forward, one step back'.

Or, sometimes, 'one step forward, two (or more) steps back'. That's the nature of change, it's how change happens. Random bad stuff happens in life, obviously, especially medical stuff; recurrences, long-term effects of cancer, or long-term effects of treatment, for example.

Once again, there are some useful questions you might wish to ponder during a time of setback:

- *What did you (and your nearest-and-dearest) do last time?*
- *Did you even know, when you first had to meet that challenge, that you could do it?*
- *What, then, did you learn about yourself and the people around you?*
- *What advice would you, when you were dealing well with things last time, give to this future you now?*
- *What would you like to notice, in the way you're dealing with this present situation, that will tell you that you have learned from last time?*

- *Who would be least surprised if you dealt well with things this time round?*

As well as these unforeseeable 'setbacks', it's also true that, 'old habits die hard'. We get used to doing things in a certain way and have certain familiar patterns of experiences over a long period of time, and it's hard to shift them. We might even notice that, by the end of a day, we're 'in a better place', but the next morning it feels like we're 'back to square one'.[176] This happens a lot.

Here are a few thoughts:

- *So, you've noticed a pattern, which means that you have developed some more expertise.*
  - *What advice can this 'expert you' give yourself?*
  - *What's going on of an evening when you're on a roll?*
  - *What do you want to remember the next morning after the night before?*
- *When do you wake up 'back at square one' and surprise yourself by getting 'back into you stride'?*
  - *What does that say about the control you do have, after all?*
  - *What do you notice about those times? For example, is it when you have to do something for someone else?*
  - *If you were to 'bottle' what it takes to get going, even when it feels like a monumental effort, what would you put on the label?*

No man is an island[177]: taking people with you

Even if we ourselves are wildly successful at change, what of the people around us? How quickly do they get used to the 'new and improved you' as you learn to live well? Do they even *want* to get to get used to the new you, if, for example, they quite like 'wrapping

---

[176] This is known as 'spontaneous recovery'.
[177] John Donne (1572-1631) *Devotions Upon Emergent Occasions, and severall steps in my Sicknes, - Meditation XVII*, 1624.

you up in cotton wool' and feeling needed themselves? Sounds like time for a conversation!

Here are some 'starters for 10':

- *I'm looking forward to [e.g., going out for walks]. What are you looking forward to?*
- *Thank you for carrying me when I needed it; I'm hoping to do more for myself again. When you were doing a lot for me, what did you enjoy? What do we both want to be doing differently from when I got ill in the first place?*
- *What things might we love to do, apart or together, that neither of us has ever got round to doing or even thought of?*
- *Suppose in a year's time we looked back at the time I started being better and realised that was the start of the best ever times:*
  - o *What are we pleased that's different?*
  - o *What would we never want to go back to?*
  - o *What would we be holding onto tightly?*
  - o *What would we be so pleased about that we would be doing even more of it?*

Sometimes lonely, but don't walk alone

Living with cancer can be an isolating experience; as if the rest of the world is at a party one is no longer invited to. If you feel that way, right now, I would invite you to (re)read common experiences in Chapter 2. You may also be interested in getting together with other people 'in the same boat' which can help you understand that you are not alone.

Naturally, a fair few people I've met are wary that such groups would be a 'moaning shop' or a 'pity party' that could make them feel worse. The obvious thing to do, then, is ask around from trusted sources. including your health professional and, in the UK, the Macmillan website[178] and the respective websites for different

---

[178] https://www.macmillan.org.uk/ accessed 10/06/2022

cancers[179]. I know from experiences that hospices offer excellent group work; if they can't help you, they will probably know someone who can.

I can also recommend the free-to-use Solution-Focused telephone helpline service 'Let's Keep Talking'[180], originated by colleagues of mine, Dr. Suzi Curtis and Mr. Steve Flatt.

Sometimes your top priorities may be material ones; again, make sure to raise it in conversations with health professionals and, if they don't 'hear' you (they should do, it's part of routine assessments in UK cancer guidance), you can approach Macmillan, Citizens' Advice Bureaux and cancer charities yourself.

Even more about bringing good from bad…

Working in the British National Health Service (NHS), you get to enjoy[181] many mandatory trainings. One of the most lasting I've yet experienced was delivered by a Transplant Co-ordinator, who talked passionately about her work, asking for relatives' permission to use organs from their deceased loved ones and encouraging colleagues to do the same. Anticipating what we were thinking, she reminded us that, for those families, the worst had already happened, and that giving life to others may be the only good thing that could bring any meaning to the situation, any sense of good out of tragedy. She reinforced the point by telling us about a medical doctor whose child's organs had not been used as no-one had broached the subject. The doctor, therefore having been denied this comfort, felt it keenly and rightly said so publicly.

---

[179] e.g. https://prostatecanceruk.org/ , https://breastcancernow.org/ …etc accessed 10/06/2022.

[180] https://workingconversationsgroup.org/lets-keep-talking/

[181] You may think this ironic. I couldn't possibly comment. My boss might be reading this.

So, in a similar way, might you be interested in 'recruiting' your personal trauma to help others? Can you bring meaning and purpose out of your struggles?

There are many ways to do this, informally and formally:

- *Is there a new depth to your compassion for your (literal and metaphorical) neighbour that will emerge in small kindnesses and make a significant difference to their life?*
- *If you are in a group of people with similar medical stories, do you feel that you can support and encourage those who are earlier on in their medical journey? Are you part of a 'cancer buddy' scheme run by your health professional?*
- *Are you involved in working with your local health professionals as a 'person with lived experience[182]' in co-designing services?*
- *Are you interested in 'sitting at the high table' with regional decision-makers who set standards, as is standard practice in Cancer Alliances[183]?*
- *Are you involved in running activities like informal groups, fundraising, etc.?*
- *What else are you doing, at whatever scale, that makes a difference, just as in the Starfish Story, above?*

Even more about not walking alone (1): agreeing the agenda with professionals[184]

In Chapter 1, I talked about how, strangely enough, both parties (yourself/your nearest-and-dearest and the health professional) in a conversation could be hemmed in by anxiety, with a sense of time

---

[182] At the time of writing, this is one of the more common descriptors of what used to be called 'expert patients'. Presumably, in a few years, there will be another epithet.

[183] In England. Mine is the Cheshire and Merseyside Cancer Alliance https://www.cmcanceralliance.nhs.uk/ accessed 10/06/2022.

[184] With thanks to Prof. Deborah Christie for her suggestion, based on reading an earlier manuscript, to write some more about how to collaborate with professionals, and some examples she shared.

running out and not being heard. If you get as far as Chapter 7, you'll also read an account of a patient's 'mixed' experiences, so you'll maybe want to keep this bit in mind.

Yes, we professionals are humans too and flawed[185]. So how can we help a conversation to be a, forgive the cliché, 'win-win' situation[186]?

Proper Preparation Prevents Pretty[187] Poor Performance (PPPPP).

Before the conversation, using the questions and principles I've mentioned before, have you:

- Asked yourself and the people who matter to you, *in advance*, what you're hoping will come from the conversation?
- Written a letter or emailed them[188], or, failing that, phoned them with your thoughts?
- Written some notes to take in with you?

Within the conversation:

- Would you benefit from an 'ally', whether personal or professional, to help you 'find your voice?'

---

[185] Ask my wife. Better still, don't.

[186] In fact, if it goes well, you'll often as not be making the choices you make jointly more effective, so you'll help shape the professional's practice for other patients and save the NHS money: a 'win-win-win'. And if you then go on to help other people too in your life, it's a 'win-win-win-win.'... ok I'll stop now. But you get the point; the right conversation sets up a virtuous circle of benefit. So, if you're reluctant to speak up, maybe remember how it's not a selfish, but a moral, thing to do.

[187] Other versions of this 'P' are available but I'm far too well bred to mention anything that rhymes with 'miss'.

[188] Generally, this means their secretary. I love it when people who see me take this initiative. In fact, in my department, we ask people, in advance, what life they're looking for. It really gets the first conversation off to a flying start; not only are we focused in the right direction, but, also, they've frequently started doing some of it and noticed they are.

- Might you benefit from recording the conversation? (Always ask in advance)
- Will you or an ally take notes?

After the conversation:

- Will you be enquiring about follow-up appointments?
- Would you like to be copied into the professionals' letters to each other? Or even wish to actively decline this? This is completely your choice.

Even more about not walking alone (2): recruiting professionals' expertise

You may have noticed I have talked a lot about the potential and strengths you, your nearest-and-dearest and kindred spirits have. This is deliberate. Traditionally, much of the writings and teachings around cancer have been written, and delivered, in a professional-centric way. This implies that the patients' role is, at best, co-operating however they can with the wisdom and knowledge of the professional. Hopefully you've read enough, given that you've got this far, to see yourself as a competent person, an expert in your own life.

What, then, of the, sometimes-crucial things that health professionals (HP) can bring to the party? How can you get the very best out of the HP? How can you get the most out of your collaboration together?

Let's start with the things they have access to that you don't, the most obvious being treatment(s), whether medical or other, for example psychological.

The NHS, from the very top level, says a lot about its person-centred values and has done for years. In a relatively early publication[189], for

---

[189] Department of Health. (2001) *The expert patient: a new approach to chronic disease management for the twenty-first century.* London: Department of Health.

example, there was much talk of patients as *"key decision-makers in the treatment process, that they should feel empowered in their relationship with health care professionals"* and that they are *"untapped resources"* of expertise.

How might then that work in reality?

What might you take with you into conversations with HPs that will help turn this high-level aspiration into your personal reality? Here are some questions[190] you might like:

- *I'm hoping to live as long as possible and I don't care what it takes. I've not had an easy life so I know how to push through things. What are my options?*
- *I really, really still want to be able to do [occupation or passionate hobby] because I'm at my best that way. Is that possible? If not all of it, what bits of it?*
- *I don't want to spend the rest of my life feeling sick and travelling for treatment. It's more about quality than quantity. Can we work around that?*
- *I don't mind a bit of pain as long as I'm still me. Have you got something that will just take the edge off it?*
- *I can't relax, and have never been good at that. Now I can't keep busy all the time as I'm too tired. I've found deep breathing helps, but have you got anything to help me relax? I've heard a lot about mindfulness…*
- *I've had some counselling before, for something else in my life; it helped. Have you got anyone like that here?*
- *In the end, I want to spend as much quality time with my family as possible because they are good for me. Can you help me do that?*

---

https://webarchive.nationalarchives.gov.uk/+/http://www.dh.gov.uk/en/Publicationsandstatistics/Publications/PublicationsPolicyAndGuidance/DH_4006801 accessed 27/06/2020

[190] These are just *some* off the top of my head from experience. There would be an infinite number of possibilities!

You will see from the above examples that the HP is being invited into a collaborative relationship with the patient. Should they choose to accept it, the HP role is re-cast from 'expert by assumption' to 'expert by *commission*', with the added element that not only might they be being invited to offer a treatment, but also to signpost, if needs be, to someone who can.

I have found, over the years, that before someone is referred to me, two of the best possible questions I can ask a HP colleague are:

- *What do you as the referrer want out of it?*
- *What does the patient want out of it?*

Collaborations between experts

In the diagram, you'll see that both you and the HP have expertise, a 'medical bag' of things that help. The aim, naturally, is for you and the HP to pool together your expertise so that you can move towards the place where you want to be.

Here is another way of representing the partnership between you and health professionals. This was produced by some long-standing colleagues of mine, one being a GP and one a Consultant Clinical Psychologist[191]:

Behaviour change in
Four steps Dr Jen Unwin

1.Can Dr and patient
agree on shared
health **goals**?

2.Explore relevant
resources and
patient **resilience**

Reflect on what is working,
sincere compliments,
successes: **noticing**

G.R.I.N!

3.Agree next small
increments
towards agreed goals

With partnership, come responsibilities

Very occasionally, a patient will say to me 'I wish I didn't know'. Sometimes this is because the professional has felt obligated to tell them absolutely everything (even though they may not want to hear it). Other times they may wish they hadn't asked!

So, my advice would be to 'be clear about what you want' and hopefully that will indeed be 'heard'.

For example[192]:

---

[191]   Unwin, D. & Unwin, J. https://bhma.org/wp-content/uploads/2019/06/ GRIN-Unwins-JHH-16.2.pdf, reproduced with authors' permission.
[192] With apologies to 'Doc Martin', ITV Television, UK (2004-2019).

Patient: Doctor, will I die?
Doctor: Yes....... but not today.

Onward and upward?

Having read the book, dear reader, has it been a good use of your time? If so, what has made it so? What will you take from this that you value? That you want to build on?

If nothing else, you'll have, hopefully, (re)learned several things; that you're persistent, you value your time, and you have at the least the beginnings of an idea of what time well spent *does* look like to you. (If nothing else, you've got something to light your barbeque with.)

One way or another, chances are that by reading this far, you're at least one step closer to living well with cancer.

Concluding thought

Once upon a time, not so very long ago, a dearly loved and missed friend of mine[193] decided to climb Kilimanjaro (like you do). Not being in the very first flush of his youth, this turned out to be hard work. He was offered some local advice that made all the difference:

The higher the mountain, the smaller the steps.

---

[193] Revd. Tim Hall

CHAPTER SIX

THE 'SOLUTION-FOCUSED' APPROACH: MORE ON WHAT IT IS (AND WHAT IT ISN'T)

'We learn, when we respect the dignity of people, that they cannot be denied the elementary right to participate fully in the solutions to their own problems. Self-respect arises only out of people who play an active part in solving their own crisis'[194]

You may wonder...

Why I haven't waxed lyrical about Cognitive-Behavioural Therapy (CBT) given that practically everyone, in the UK at least, will have heard of it. The short answer is that, at least for me, it doesn't fit nearly so well as a solution-focused approach. More on both follows.

Solution-Focused approaches: the 'under the bonnet' stuff

Although, as we know, elements of SF discussed throughout this book (such as 'counting ones' blessings') have been around a long time, in its modern form, SF really got going in the 1980s with the work of Steve de Shazer et al.[195].

SF is specifically cited as the approach of choice in key cancer guidance, most notably in *Improving Supportive and Palliative Care for Adults with Cancer (NICE, 2004)[196]*.

---

[194] Alinsky, S.D. (2010) *Rules for Radicals* (reissue ed). London: Vintage.
[195] See, for example, amongst many, de Shazer, S. (1994) *Words Were Originally Magic*. NY: Norton.
[196] https://www.nice.org.uk/guidance/csg4 accessed 10/06/2022

It also appears in related guidance on the personalisation of approaches in healthcare, such as *Personalised Care and Support Planning*[197]. Quite recently, NHS England has published some very helpful guides on what a personalised approach really looks like, which, although not specifically citing SF, are replete with the language of 'what matters to you'[198].

Building on previous chapters, here are some more musings on what makes the solution-focused approach what it is:

(i) The power of focusing on the future

Focusing on your very particular, wished-for future can yield great results. This is for several reasons:

Firstly, it makes sense to pay attention to where you want to get to. Why go from A to B via Z? If you don't have to go 'round the houses', it's a lot easier to maintain momentum and hope. As noted in Chapter 3, 'If you don't know where the hole is, it's going to be a long day on the golf course'[199].

Secondly, while reading this, or indeed while having a conversation with somebody else, maybe take a moment to notice a few things about yourself, When you do, do you begin to sit up straighter, are you smiling? As you work (and it does take work) on imagining how you would really like things to be in the future, do you look upwards rather than at your feet? Chances are that you are already unleashing the power of your imagination, the same power that enables you to begin to believe in yourself, often by remembering what you already

---

[197] Coalition for Collaborative Care/ NHS England, (2015, accessed 10/06/2022). Personalised Care and Support Planning.
https://www.england.nhs.uk/ourwork/patient-participation/patient-centred/c4cc/
[198] https://www.england.nhs.uk/publication/personalised-care-factsheets/ (accessed 10/06/2022)
[199] Hoyt, M. (1996) A Golfer's Guide to Brief Therapy in Constructive Therapies 2. Guildford Press.

know about yourself. You're (re-)discovering that good old-fashioned thing—hope.

So, even when, or perhaps *especially* when, the problem (e.g., anxiety) has become a solid concrete wall blocking all possible progress, think about this; what does it look like on the other side of the wall? When you do that, you'll begin to notice that the wall's not so solid after all. There are cracks, holes even. All bets are on again. And notice your sense of hope, however small.

A third good reason for asking, or being asked these questions, is that, sometimes, a future-focus is one of the few things that is going to work! It may be with, say, anxiety, that there is no obvious quick fix because being anxious about cancer's possible reoccurrence *is* rational, as we have discussed in Chapter 2. But, and here's the best bit, sometimes there is also *no obvious connection between what does in fact work and the problem* (anxiety in this case). The individual who is trying to help with the anxiety, be it a professional or otherwise, is unlikely to suggest[200] that the answer to concern about cancer is washing your car. Or watching gory true-crime TV. Or building a tepee[201]. Is anyone, rational at least, likely to "prescribe" building a fully-functioning[202] Dalek for a man with intense, chronic pain[203]. I've obviously quoted some of the idiosyncratic examples I've known.

Generally, though, as noted earlier the answer is very often 'grandchildren' or 'dogs'. You might still get there if you use CBT. However, by using SF questioning, these things emerge quite quickly and, crucially, are 'owned' by the patient. They're not immediately predictable when the concern is first identified.

---

[200] Unless of course they happened to be psychic. Now that would be an interesting book.

[201] All real examples.

[202] Minus the laser cannon.

[203] Another real example. Unfortunately, it was my close colleague who had that particular conversation. 15 years down the line, the gentleman in question is still going strong; he co-runs expert patient groups with us.

Fundamentally, the question is often: 'what brings you 'joy'?'

Thinking about it, once more, I remember talked to a distressed elderly lady in a hospice and she talked fondly of the children she'd taught to sing in her Sunday School.

Successfully engaging with one's wished-for future requires one to 'park' the intuitive assumption that the more one 'attacks' a problem head-on, the more successful one is. This habit of 'striving' is especially difficult to step away from if one has that disposition in the first place; sometimes the most earnest people—the conscientious ones with an eye for detail coupled with a strong work ethic—do struggle.

People of certain occupations—for example, medical doctors, nurses, engineers[204], police, solicitors and teachers—I've noticed tend to launch themselves into a quest for explanations and control. Whether it's because that's the way they're trained to think, or whether people who think that way are attracted to those professions, or both, is not clear. It's just something I've noticed over the years…

Einstein is often mis-credited with the saying 'the definition of insanity is doing the same thing and expecting a different result'[205]. Nonetheless, for some, it's difficult to disengage from this self-defeating quest, often because *it's the only model they know.* Furthermore, trying something else could look to them, or those around them, as not trying hard enough; a kind of moral failure.

So… if you can, keep the faith… it can reward richly.

---

[204] …..other professions of course may recognise themselves…

[205] Research online suggests that the first time this quote was used word-for-word was in Rita Mae Brown's 1983 novel *Sudden Death* (Bantam Books, NY.) No one is entirely sure where it originated through—as alternative wordings are rife.

(ii) The right conversation enables the emergence of solutions: *timing is everything*

In earlier chapters, I introduced a graph that reflects the pattern I so often see in conversations.

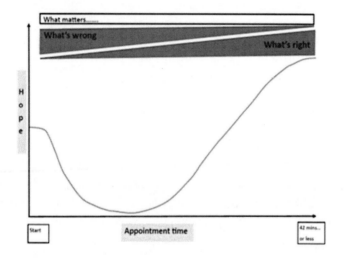

Here is the full sequence:

Typically, during the early part of an appointment, whilst listening out all the while for what matters[206] to the patient and what's right[207] in their world, I hear a lot about *what's wrong*, as represented by the top left of the blue area. This is fair enough, as it's their chance to be heard, especially if they haven't been particularly well listened to by professionals or wider society! As you'll see, the red line (the sense of hope in the room) goes down for a time.

---

[206] See Chapter 3
[207] See Chapter 4

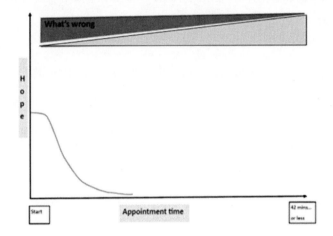

Maybe it's largely my hope which begins to plummet. People, at some level, know another story about themselves, and have some sense of their own resilience even if the right moment in the appointment hasn't yet arrived when they're ready to share this alternative story. This is, after all, their 'day in court'.

However, there's more to be learned even at this stage and more for me to listen out for. What they share as being 'not right' gives significant clues as to what they would like to be right, which, in the end, is what matters to them. For example:

P: My husband never hangs the sheets out properly.[208]

P: Everyone I know is just getting on with their own lives.

P: I just don't go out, it's like Groundhog Day all over again.

It's not a great leap to imagine that, in those examples, the patient would want (respectively) to resume their former position as launderer-in-chief, to feel connection with others, and get out more.

---

[208] I hear this a lot (at work, I mean)!

Then it's a question of timing. Taking the last, one might come back with:

H: So…you'd like to go out more?

Which, if it lands well, may reward us with something like:

P: Yes… it may sound silly, but I miss just popping out to Tesco.

Of course, it may not land well and, in which case, the patient may rebut this with:

P: Of course, I would but it's way too difficult to, so I'm stuck.

This rather suggests the timing was off. The conversation was not at the point where **P** could even bring themselves to express their hope.

Hence, it seems the conversation has to 'rewind' to an earlier stage:

P: I just don't go out, it's like Groundhog Day all over again.

H: You're not going out? That sounds rubbish. What does it take to get through each day?

The point that I'd like to make here, under the SF bonnet, is that it's all a question of choreography and timing. A mis-step which leaves the patient behind can set things back. But this is not irredeemable. I've even found myself saying to patients when they give me an indication that I have got it wrong:

H: It doesn't sound like that was a great question! What would have been a better question?

Sometimes the conversation might have to stay in this 'place' for some time. I've learnt over the years that some patients have very good reasons to be mistrustful; maybe a significant individual in their lives has let them down, or even damaged them. Maybe professionals were over-eager to discharge them and pounced upon the first positive thing they said to suggest they could stop being there for them. So, it's important to make 'the charitable assumption' that people are doing their very best unless, and until, proved otherwise[209].

Hopefully, it will be clear from this description that SF practice is not 'problem-phobic', as some critics would have it. Patients will, inevitably, talk about what's wrong. The SF method's 'article of faith' is that by keeping a particular type of conversation going, especially one that doesn't insist that talking about problems is always necessary for improvement, 'what's right' will emerge. So, the chances are that, by staying in step with the patient, the curve will start to go upwards. After all, the vast majority of people who come forward for help do so because they want something out of this help and they are motivated to succeed.

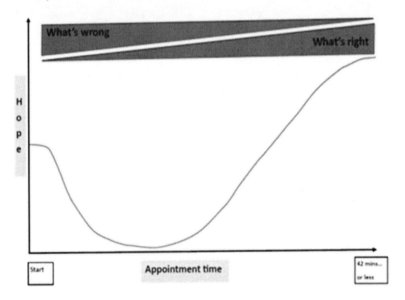

In addition, as noted above, even when patients are talking about 'what's wrong', 'what matters' is becoming evident. It becomes further evident when, if the timing is right and the patient feels

---

[209] Once again, I would credit The Brief Group, London, formerly known as the Brief Therapy Practice for teaching me this.

genuinely listened to, the SF practitioner employs the future-focused questions described in Chapter 3.

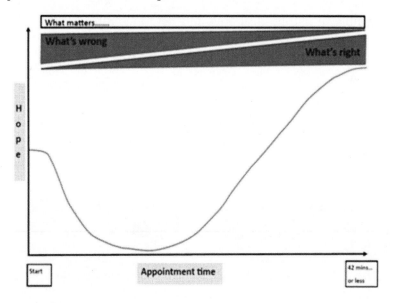

As described in the section above, the very act of conjuring up a vision of the life we would hope for, a life full of what matters to us (whatever that may be), more often than not has some 'magic' of its own[210]. Sometimes, quite unexpectedly, we start to spontaneously remember moments when some elements of this vision of the future, however fleetingly, have already begun to happen. This relentless listening, even what we might call 'extreme listening'[211], really pays dividends.

Which brings us onto....

---

[210] Steve de Shazer, one of the founders of this approach titled his book 'Words were originally magic'

[211] I did at least *co-invent* this term, using the analogy of extreme sports that go off-piste... See Bliss, E. and Bray, D. *The smallest solution focused particles*. Journal of Systemic Therapies 28 (2) 62-74.

(iii) Positive Selective Abstraction

(Or in everyday language: 'nothing succeeds like success')

From CBT theory, we notice one mechanism that tends towards low mood and diminished lives; the *depressogenic cycle*. This is where people ruminate on what's wrong and lose their ability to see things in a balanced way and, therefore, problem-solve. This is closely allied to negative selective abstraction, in which, without any conscious effort, people only notice the bad news, the 'downside' about themselves, the world and the future. They enlarge the bad and downplay the good.

You'll see, then, that we are inviting patients to do the very opposite here, to pay attention to what they really want and to their successes. This, however, is not to deny that problems exist, but, instead, to assert that these problems tend to co-exist with solutions. Like sunshine and showers in our, ahem, beloved British weather. And it turns out to be more useful to consciously pay attention to instances of what matters happening than to forget about them. To use another analogy, it works better to notice the doughnut rather than just the hole![212]

(iv) An offer that may interest you

A little while ago, I authored an online interactive tool for audiologists to learn how to use SF for people with tinnitus[213].

This enables practitioners to experience contrasting conversations: problem-focused /advice-driven ones versus solution-focused ones. We (in Southport, UK) are also developing one locally for people living with chronic pain. If you're interested, please get in touch via

---

[212] Interested lay people and professionals may wish to read a piece by a doctor colleague: Blayney, S (2014) 'Survival as medical registrar on call: remember the doughnut', *Clinical Medicine*, Vol 14, No 5: 506–9

[213] British Tinnitus Association https://www.tinnitus.org.uk/ accessed 10/06/2022

the QR code, below, and I would be happy to provide you with more information:[214]

(v) ...but here's something for now: the very anatomy of a solution-focused conversation

I'm currently developing a similar online interactive learning tool for cancer practitioners with a focus on helping people with cancer-related anxiety[215]. Again, if you're interested, please scan the QR code below[216]:

Below, you'll find a flow diagram[217], which will form the basis of the script driving the interactive tool. It systematically sets out how such conversations typically proceed, concluding at different points,

---

[214] This QR code will send an email to me (Dominic) directly and I will be happy to send you the materials. Your information will not be kept, stored or shared with any third party.

[215] I just need to get round to filming it...

[216] This QR code is to register to receive this information when the tool is ready (if it is not already by the time you read this). Your information will be saved for the sole purpose of providing this information and will not be shared with any third party.

[217] Produced on Lucidchart

crucially depending on the choices the professional makes within the conversation.

Problems with *problem-based* approaches:

As I mused at the beginning of the chapter, you may be wondering why I haven't dived into the benefits of Cognitive-Behavioural Therapy (CBT) given its popularity. The short answer is that, at least for me, it doesn't fit as well as a solution-focused approach. A long answer would also include a questioning of its domination in the NHS and its evidence-base[218], together with philosophical objections to its insistence on the expertise of the therapist and the application of what is in effect a medical (as in 'illness') model. An even longer answer would include reference to the way that even CBT is itself changing, referencing strengths, resilience, etc., increasingly in new variants of itself[219], presumably because that works better. Here are some more thoughts on the problems with CBT and similar approaches:

(i) 'Paralysis by analysis' and feeding the problem.

I've noticed over the years that some people of an analytical persuasion, 'over-thinkers' as they are sometimes called (and call themselves), 'disappear down a rabbit hole' and the anxiety or other psychological problem becomes worse. This is not because they are not trying; it's for the opposite of reasons. They are most certainly trying, but not in a way that seems to work. This is akin to someone trying very hard to fall asleep. By applying ever-increasing focus to the problem, in an earnest quest for an answer, it is as if they are, quite inadvertently (and to use a metaphor from the theatre), 'building

---

[218] Here are some excellent references for the enthusiast: Dalal, F. (2019) *CBT: The Cognitive Behavioural Tsunami: Managerialism, Politics, and the Corruptions of Science*. Abingdon: Routledge; Jackson, C. & Rizq, R. (2019) *The Industrialisation of Care: counselling, psychotherapy and the impact of IAPT*. Monmouth: PCCS Books.

[219] Have a look at an excellent book for much more on this: Bannink (2012) *Practicing Positive CBT: From Reducing Distress to Building Success* Chichester: Wiley-Blackwell.

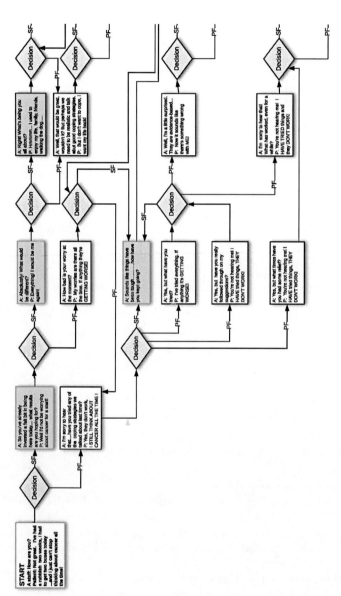

Cancer (anxiety) flowchart for online training in solution-focused versus problem-focused conversations.
Dominic.Bray@nhs.net 25/11/2019

The 'solution-focused' approach: more on what it is (and what it isn't)

SEMI-IMPROVISED SF CONVERSATION to include uncovering more strengths and other elements such as:
- what's their life?
- when else does that happen?
- what else do you do that works?
- developing a joint plan like a good HNA, based on what each needs to do.

A: What do you notice about yourself, and what does he notice about you?
P: I'm more like me again!

A: I expect the worry is better when you do that?
P: My worry is there all the time, if anything, it's GETTING WORSE!

Decision — SF / PF

A: What do you do with him?
P: We play trains and tell jokes.

A: What's stopping you doing that?
P: My worry is there all the time. If anything, it's GETTING WORSE!

Decision — SF / PF

A: Who would be the first to notice our work together had made a difference?
P: Hmmmm.....my 5 year old grandson Sam.... I'd spend more time with him.

A: Yes of course.....tell me more about that.
P: Hmmmm..... I used to enjoy my life, family, friends, walking the dog,.....

A: I can see why you'd feel that way. But the evidence tells us most people find coping strategies work.
P: But I'm NOT MOST PEOPLE. If you don't mind me asking, do you have a lot of experience in this field or are you working from a book

P: Well, you have to don't you? It's not just about me. It's not fair on the family if I just give up.

A: I'm sorry that's really not what it means. Sounds like things have been tough...where's kept you going?

A: Well, I wouldn't say that, but most people find something works.
P: But I'm NOT MOST PEOPLE. If you don't mind me asking, do you have a lot of experience in this field or are you working from a book

A: I'm sorry I missed that. Sounds like things have been tough...what's kept you going?

A: Well, there's a little something. Maybe people find something works.
P: But I'm NOT MOST PEOPLE. If you don't mind me asking, do you have a lot of experience in this field or are you working from a book

P: No, I'll sorry, I'm afraid, with respect, this isn't your area.

A: I'm sorry you feel that way. Sounds like things have been tough...how have you kept going?

A: With respect, I have seen many patients like yourself, I wouldn't have known. This isn't working.
[folds arms] Now I'm angry. I'm not having till I get proper help!

Decision — SF / PF

[OPTION ON SCREEN, NOT ROLE PLAYED] Offer to refer on?

[OPTION ON SCREEN, NOT ROLE PLAYED] Offer to see again?

[OPTION ON SCREEN, NOT ROLE PLAYED] Discharge to referrer?

[OPTION ON SCREEN, NOT ROLE PLAYED] Offer to see him again?

[OPTION ON SCREEN, NOT ROLE PLAYED] Show him the door?

[OPTION ON SCREEN, NOT ROLE PLAYED] Call Security?

[OPTION ON SCREEN, NOT ROLE PLAYED] Refer to Psychologist?

[WHAT APPEARS ON SCREEN, NOT ROLE PLAYED] Your working relationship is broken so patient may or may not agree

[WHAT APPEARS ON SCREEN, NOT ROLE PLAYED] Your working relationship is broken so patient unlikely to accept, less attend

[WHAT APPEARS ON SCREEN, NOT ROLE PLAYED] Wait for formal complaint

[WHAT APPEARS ON SCREEN, NOT ROLE PLAYED] Patient unlikely to accept, less attend

[WHAT APPEARS ON SCREEN, NOT ROLE PLAYED] Wait for formal complaint

[WHAT APPEARS ON SCREEN, NOT ROLE PLAYED] Wait for formal complaint

[WHAT APPEARS ON SCREEN, NOT ROLE PLAYED] Consider retraining in a less stressful occupation like bomb disposal?

[WHAT APPEARS ON SCREEN, NOT ROLE PLAYED] You don't like your approach. Would you like to start the whole simulation again?

[WHAT APPEARS ON SCREEN, NOT ROLE PLAYED] Show the door. Refer back to GP for community-based IAPT (Improving Access to Psychology Therapies) service.

up its part' so it becomes increasingly 'centre stage' in their awareness. This is, unfortunately, one of the dangers of approaches that invite people to spend a lot of time paying attention to their psychological problem.

By way of contrast, SF approaches don't assume that the problems need to be centre-stage in any conversation; in a manner of speaking, then, problems are starved, rather than fed.

(ii) Having struggles don't make you 'mentally ill'.

Greater minds than I have written extensively about the colonisation of people's lives by therapies[220], whereby ordinary, completely understandable experiences are labelled as being pathological and in need of a particular kind of 'therapy-ing'. (Hopefully from Chapters 1 and 2, you will have seen I don't see it that way. 'There but for the grace of God etc....'[221]). The danger with this school of thought, of course, is that if you come to believe you have a profound and insoluble problem that needs a particular, specialised kind of outside help, that becomes a reality.

Ironically, CBT theory would agree; if your beliefs in your own ability to deal with troubling thoughts/situations, also known as secondary appraisals, get damaged, that becomes a problem in itself. If you absorb other people's messaging that you are a non-coper, that becomes a self-fulfilling prophecy.

SF approaches, as I say, belong more to the 'There but for the grace of God go I...'[222] school of thought. Any one of us might well feel and react similarly in similar circumstances. If anything, the SF practitioner is highly curious about how the individual concerned has coped as well as they have and stopped things getting even worse!

---

[220] E.g. Dalal, F. (2019) *CBT: The Cognitive Behavioural Tsunami: Managerialism, Politics, and the Corruptions of Science.* Abingdon: Routledge
[221] Attributed to John Bradford (circa 1510-1555).
[222] Attributed to John Bradford (circa 1510-1555).

(iii) When is a problem not a problem? The pitfalls of monitoring for its *absence*...

Supposing you have cancer-related anxiety, a fear of recurrence (Chapter 2), and, quite naturally, you want it to go away. How do you know a problem is still there when you are not thinking about it? It is probably something like that saying "If a tree falls in a forest and no one is around to hear it, does it make a sound?"[223]

This is more than a philosophical dead end. Supposing we take the view that the problem, in this case anxiety, is always there. We may try and disprove it by monitoring when it is not there. Unfortunately, this is akin to opening the fridge door to see if the light has gone off. The very act of looking for improvement, in the sense of *the absence of a problem*, brings about the very thing that one is monitoring for[224].

You may say (as people do) 'but it's always there *at the back of my mind'*. How do you know? But more to the point (should you wish to think this one through), that means that you could have an infinite number of problems lurking in the back of your mind that will always be a menace because you now believe you can't know they've gone. Maybe this is true, maybe it's not. The question is, however, is this useful? Is that the basis on which you want to live your life? Telling yourself you are merely sugar-coating your 'deep-seated' problems and, therefore, all experiences of wellbeing are not to be trusted and are, at best, temporary?

Further, some forms of therapy may claim that only an *expert* (i.e., not yourself) can really know what is going on inside your head. SF approaches, by way of contrast, characterise appointments as co-constructed meetings between experts; if your considered view is that your life is better, it most likely is. and the trick is to leave it at that

---

[223] Berkeley (1685- 1753); e.g. N. Warburton (2011), *A Little History of Philosophy.* Yale University Press, p87.

[224] You can impress your friends by naming Heisenberg's principle: that one cannot be an observer without affecting what one is observing

rather than being caught up with an unanswerable question about whether the problem in your head has truly gone.

Very similar principles apply to the experience of pain. When people look out for it, it's generally there (particularly when cancer has been involved in someone's life [see Chapter 2—hypervigilance]). One could, even in their better moments, say *'well, I had a better day, but the pain was always there'*. It's like 'yes, butting' yourself. Are you going to potentially rob yourself of joy by insisting that the pain is always there, even when you're not 'consciously' aware of it? If you find yourself doing this on a regular basis, you may need to ask yourself whether you feel other people are not taking your plight seriously, so quite naturally you're having to emphasise your problems to get them to listen. Or maybe you're still 'grieving' (see Chapter 1) and not quite ready to embrace a 'both/and' life where problems do happen some (or even a lot) of the time which you will need to, and can, find a way to 'work round' towards a thriving future.

(iii) The Mislabelling / Demoting of Solutions

Relatedly, in the course of SF training and MDT meetings, colleagues have occasionally alluded to the solutions patients come up with as 'distractions'. I have two sorts of concerns about this: philosophical and spiritual, both of which are to do with ultimate (dis)benefit to the patients.

Taking the first, asserting that what the patient is engaged in (or has decided to do) is a 'distraction' is an assumption that makes the potentially enjoyable or even joyful activity they're engaged in into an epiphenomenon, a side-show, to the 'real', main event. As argued above, this is unprovable, and worse (extending the metaphor of the patient's life as a play in which they are the lead character), this builds up the 'part' of the problem.

Secondly, in what sense is the joy experienced in the company, say, of grandchildren, or dogs, or in the act of communing with nature, adequately described as a distraction? Perhaps 'being fully alive' would be a better description?

So, instead, according to the SF approach, your mission (should you choose to accept it) is to monitor for *wellbeing*. That is, to look out for, and, if needs be, measure, improvements in the features of one's own life that one most values: time, experiences of purpose, of joy, love and all those other things that make life worth living. Put it this way, one can absolutely notice and measure improvements. Chances are, when those wonderful things are happening, the experience of anxiety and/or pain will be less. But learning to trust that idea can take a while.

This is another example of the difference between the medical model (otherwise known as the 'pathological' or 'illness' model [as exemplified by standard CBT]) and a more collaborative approach. The medical model assumes that a lot of identifying, measuring and targeting problems is not just important, but arguably a necessary step towards the eradication. Unfortunately, as we have seen, this can be counterproductive[225]. Instead, a collaborative or narrative model is, in a sense, about re-authoring one's life and working towards

---

[225] If you've got nothing better to do, here is one (a published paper) we prepared earlier: Bray, D. et al. (2015) ''First, do no harm': a solution-focused approach to pain measurement and management'. *European Journal of Palliative Care.* 22(4) 190-193.

living that preferred future (that being the 'happy ending' that we would wish for, whether the ending will be today or years ahead). Rather than a constant recourse to problems, one 'boldly goes' (as Captain James T. Kirk would say) into the future.

(iv) A bit more about CBT/IAPT

In the UK, governments of various persuasions have, for some years, taken the view that the large bulk of psychological help should be delivered by a mechanism called Increasing Access to Psychological Therapies (IAPT), which is delivered by various organisations in different localities. It makes no bones about the fact that, with a referral to IAPT you likely get CBT. You are most unlikely, at least 'officially'[226], to be offered a Solution-Focused approach. You may wish to make up your own mind on the justification for this. I will note that, however, in much of the NHS, including where I work, we are required to collect the 'Family and Friends Test'. This really gets to the heart of the matter because it asks whether you would want your nearest and dearest to experience that service. This information is publicly available. To the best of my knowledge, IAPT doesn't publish the results of the Family and Friends test, at least prominently[227].

Never the Twain?

Clearly, we should not 'throw the baby out with the bathwater'! There are things out there that help, which health professionals either have access to or can point patients towards.

But before we get onto that, a word (if I may) about *context*. Clever techniques, equipment and the like are all very well, but without a shared understanding between patients and professionals, they will

---

[226] I say this as I know a fair number of people who work for, or have worked for, an IAPT service and, thankfully, I hear a lot about how they at least bend the rules, if not break them. In summary, the bulk of IAPT workers are supposed to follow a manual. From what I've heard, many don't.
[227] https://www.england.nhs.uk/mental-health/adults/iapt/ (accessed 10/06/2022)

often be wasted[228]. As described towards the end of Chapter 5, what doesn't work is 'expertise by *assumption*', that is, if the professional working with you prescribes or suggests things when:

- They don't fit, either because they don't get you to where you would want to be or they are simply impractical;
- They are disrespectful, either because they are (often a poorer version of) what you can and should do for yourself, or they are made before you have been properly listened to, and the timing is just wrong.

You may have noticed that, particularly in Chapter 2, I referred to some 'well-known' psychological experiences, thereby potentially assuming I might be the expert in what's good for you!

So, notwithstanding everything above, there will very likely be things that are on offer from a range of professionals, psychological or not, that *could* be helpful. There's a lot of good *Mindfulness* work in a variety of contexts, such as alternative therapies delivered at holistic centres. CBT itself is clearly 'not entirely without virtue'[229]. And the stuff I talk about in Chapter 2; sometimes known as 'psycho-education'.

In sum, the Solution-Focused message is simple: you are the expert in your own life.

No other human[230] should assume they are more of an expert in you than you are. Hence, question everything and everyone. Ask yourself:

---

[228] Approximately 50% of all medication prescribed by the NHS is wasted; see, for example, Royal Pharmaceutical Society of Great Britain (1997). *From compliance to concordance: Towards shared goals in medicine taking.* London: Royal Pharmaceutical Society of Great Britain.
[229] Dalal, F. (2019) *CBT: The Cognitive Behavioural Tsunami: Managerialism, Politics, and the Corruptions of Science.* Abingdon: Routledge
[230] I introduce the term 'human' as people of faith like myself would believe God knows them best of all, but that's another book!

- *What really does matter to you?*
- *What expertise do you already have in getting there?*
- *Are you interested in commissioning other people's expertise to help you along the way? If so, how will you know when it's been helpful? What might, in the end, they themselves learn from you?*

Here endeth the lesson!

CHAPTER SEVEN

FROM THE HORSE'S MOUTH –
A DOCTOR'S SECOND OPINION

Introduction

I'm not a real doctor. That is, I'm not a medical doctor, but I am a Professor whose PhD title is often specified on my air tickets and hotel bookings arranged by overseas institutions. This can sometimes be to my advantage as it's gained me upgraded seats on planes, upgraded rooms in hotels and upgraded respect from doctors I've had the misfortune to visit on my travels. I've also been asked to deliver a baby on a plane and been bombarded with medical jargon by doctors assuming I was one of them.

Normally, I'm anonymous when I enter a doctor's room or receive a doctor at my bedside and I'm still anonymous (and often disturbed) when the interview is over. From reading this sentence you've probably worked out that I'm going to complain about doctors' frequent inability to treat their patients with the respect, patience and support they deserve as fellow human beings. You're right: I am. I'm also, I hope, going to be understanding of the pressures that doctors are working under, to acknowledge that there are many caring and respectful doctors and to be positive in my suggestions for improvement. First of all, though, I'd like to tell you a true story of something that happened to me recently when visiting a local hospital.

They Made Us Smile

Recently, I drove ten miles to a hospital for a consultation with a doctor. I was feeling low because it was early in the morning and I'd been up late working on a virtual lecture I was going to deliver for a university in California. I wasn't thinking of the lecture, though, as I drove, but of the swelling around the slowly healing hole where my skin graft hadn't taken, of the rodent ulcer I was waiting to be excised, of the eight new growths I'd discovered on my body, of the cystoscopy I was waiting for, of the colonoscopy I was waiting for, of the hernia repair I was waiting for and of the postponed appointment to check on my two replaced hips and my one replaced knee. I wasn't feeling at my cheerful best.

When I got to the hospital, I was relieved when I eventually found a parking space and didn't need to scream and shout. The problem, though, was I'd arrived early and, because of COVID-19, I'd no longer be able to sit in a waiting room enjoying my novel. I couldn't sit in the car because the sun was bursting in and even my 50+ sunscreen, my lip cream, my sun protected hat from Australia, my sunglasses and my sun protected snood wouldn't protect me enough from the possibility of another melanoma. So I stood in the shade outside the hospital for half an hour trying not to breathe in the fumes of passing cars or the smoke from nervous smokers. Then I put on my Liverpool FC face mask, walked into the hospital trying to avoid contagion and climbed the stairs to avoid lift phobia and congestion.

I waited briefly alone and relieved before being summoned into the doctor's room. He was seated at his desk, but, when he saw me, he greeted me by name and introduced himself. Then he smiled, warm and reassuring, and gave me the impression that he would have shaken hands if we'd been allowed to. 'You seem to have had a rough time recently', he began without any need to read from my notes. He knew about my problems and sympathised. Then he asked me how I was coping and listened patiently when I told him. Not only did he listen, but he responded with his eyes and smiled when I told him that Liverpool winning the Premier League and the occasional pint had seen me through. Only then did he focus on the reason for my visit. He knew without checking that I'd pointed out a white mark on my lower lip to a number of GPs, to numerous dermatologists, to my plastic surgeon, to a consultant following up my wide excision and lymph node biopsy and to two consultants I'd insisted on seeing on finding out after my £70 taxi ride to a distant hospital that my appointment had been cancelled without my knowledge. Now at last I had an appointment with a specialist.

He was genuinely sympathetic and examined my lips very carefully. 'I don't think that's anything to worry about,' he concluded, 'probably just a sunspot from all your years in the tropics. We'll keep an eye on it though just in case.' We had a little chat and he told me he hoped Liverpool would have a good season and I'd enjoy my beer (or words to that effect), before saying that he'd see me again later in the year.

I walked to the car park beaming. I'd just had a consultation with a senior consultant who treated me with respect, who treated me as an equal, who was professional but supportive, who laughed and joked with me and who made me feel good. In a long lifetime of hospital visits all over the world, this was a rare and treasured experience. As I drove carefully home, it reminded me of a text I'd used in a lecture about how to develop language learning materials which are driven by potentially engaging texts. As I drove, I remembered actually crying as I read the text aloud to a large audience at a conference in Malaysia.

The text is from Barr (2004)[231]. I took it from a coursebook published by two of my ex-students and added my own activities which focused on engagement and problem solving. The coursebook is by McCullagh and Wright (2008)[232]. I'd recommend this book not only to medical practitioners whose first language isn't English, but to those who are native speakers of English too.

In the text, Dr Barr talks about his interest in how long doctors typically take before interrupting patients when they are reporting their symptoms. He refers to a study which revealed that female doctors typically interrupted after three minutes, whereas male doctors could only restrain themselves for 47 seconds. After seeing these data, Dr Barr decided that he wouldn't interrupt his next patient

---

[231] Barr, D. A. (2004). 'Time to listen'. *Annals of Internal Medicine*, 41-44.
[232] McCullagh, M. & Wright, R. (2008). *Good practice: communication skills in English for the medical practitioner*. Cambridge: Cambridge University Press.

at all, but would let them talk for as long as necessary. His next
patient was a lady in her seventies. She rambled on about somebody
at work noticing something wrong, her sister telling her to go to the
doctors, the weather being awful lately and often about a cough. Dr
Barr waited, his nurse came in to point to her watch and the 'old lady'
continued for twenty-two minutes. The word 'cough' reoccurred
many times and the doctor suspected a lung problem. He sent her to
see a specialist who confirmed that she was probably suffering from
an advanced stage of lung cancer. When she returned to Dr Barr for
antibiotics, he told her about the 'grave prognosis she faced' and said
to her, 'It hasn't been a very good day for you, has it?' She smiled at
Dr Barr, reached out for his hand and patted him on his wrist. Then
she said:

'Oh, don't worry about all that. I've had a good life. But I just wanted
you to know—this is the best doctor visit it I've ever had. You're the
only one who ever listened.'

I was happy because my doctor not only gave me good news, but did
so in a way which respected me as a person. Dr Barr's patient was
happy because, although her doctor gave her bad news, he actually
listened to her. Surely this suggests how important it is that doctors
are respectful to their patients and give them time to speak. This
could possibly achieve much more than hastily prescribed medicines.
As Youngson (2012)[233] says about doctors:

> When we are grumpy, intolerant, resentful, fatigued and unhappy,
> we infect others with those feelings. When we are light-hearted,
> open, happy, caring and compassionate, we help to heal those around
> us.

> Many of us are very practised in the art of conveying busyness. The
> quick movements, brisk attention to clinical tasks, lack of eye
> contact, and clipped speech all portray a powerful message: I'm here
> for you in a strictly limited role, I'm not going to connect with you,
> and I don't have time for questions or concerns.

---

[233] Youngson, R. (2012). *Time to care.: How to love your patients and your
job*. Raglan, New Zealand: Rebelheart Publishers.

The manner in which we reveal our mental state and attitudes are almost completely non-verbal—our facial expressions, tone of voice, eye contact and body language. This means that we have all the time in the world to convey an attitude of care, kindness, and compassion even when we are busy performing clinical tasks.

But then there are patients waiting impatiently to be seen and pressures building up.

Other Experiences

Unlike Dr Barr's patient, I've had a few doctors who've actually listened to and respected me. There's one in my current GP practice and one I visited recently in a local clinic. And I can remember one in Hobart, one in Penang and one in Liverpool. But then I've lived in thirty-five different places in the UK and around the world and I've had appointments in relation to recurrent malaria, dengue fever, dysentery, shingles, an ongoing prostate problem, two hip replacements, a knee replacement, reflux, a gall bladder removal, a hiatus hernia, two inguinal hernias, severe back and neck pains, a melanoma, a variety of pre-cancerous and cancerous growths, a skin graft which didn't take, a lymph node biopsy which caused a septic leg and anxiety and depression as well. Some doctors have treated me with respect (especially when discovering that I'm a Professor) and some have been tolerable, but many have been blunt, impatient, dismissive, uninterested, unsociable, unsympathetic, sceptical, uninformative, superior, without empathy, without compassion or downright rude. I always try to be understanding of the pressures that doctors are working under and to be pleasant, informative and concise, but more often than not I come out of a doctor's room feeling worse than when I went in. There's a lot of talk at the moment about the poor mental health of people around the world and especially in such depressed places as the United Kingdom and the USA. Doctors talk about the need for people to be aware of their symptoms and to make appointments to discuss them. But when we go to have these discussions, we're often offered dangerous drugs or unreliable therapies when willingness to listen and an establishment of empathy could be much more effective. There's also a lot of talk about people who are suffering symptoms (especially men) being scared to go to the doctor and letting their symptoms get worse and worse before plucking up the courage to go. Maybe this is because they don't want to be belittled, to be in a one-sided conversation over which they have no control, to be made to think they are a nuisance wasting the doctor's time or to be treated without respect.

Here are a few of the things that doctors have said to me over the years, some of them in the UK and some of them overseas. See if you can guess what sort of doctors said them and where they were said.

Utterances
1 I'd recommend circumcision and carpet slippers.
2 I'm just letting you know they'll give you an HIV test in the middle of the night and if it's positive they'll deport you in the morning.
3 Why have you come here? I'm going home in five minutes. You should go to your GP.
4 There's nothing wrong with you.
5 If you refuse to get on the bed, there's nothing I can do for you.
6 Why are you here? This is for emergencies.

And here are the answers:

Utterances	Doctors
1 I'd recommend circumcision and carpet slippers.	A doctor in a GP surgery who I'd gone to see about a severe pain in my groin.
2 I'm just letting you know they'll give you an HIV test in the middle of the night and if it's positive they'll deport you in the morning.	A doctor in a hospital visiting my bed in the middle of the night.
3 Why have you come here? I'm going home in five minutes. You should go to your GP.	A doctor in a hospital which specialised in treating tropical diseases and which I'd been told to visit if I developed any symptoms of malaria.
4 There's nothing wrong with you.	GPs and consultants in many countries (including the UK) who've investigated my painful and frequent urination problem.
5 If you refuse to get on the bed, there's nothing I can do for you.	A doctor in an A&E Department where I'd been taken with horrendous back pain.
6 Why are you here? This is for emergencies.	A consultant in a hospital where I'd been taken by ambulance with a high fever.

Here are some more things which doctors have said to me which I found disturbing:

7 You're not my only patient you know.	GPs and consultants all over the world annoyed that my description of my symptoms was taking up too much of their time.
8 Make another appointment to discuss that.	Many GPs who refused to discuss two ailments in one visit.
9 It wasn't the best of results.	A surgeon during a follow-up telephone appointment after a procedure had gone horribly wrong.
10 You have to take a test. If you fail it, I won't do the operation.	A consultant I'd gone to see about a possible knee replacement.
11 What's wrong with you?	Many doctors on greeting me.
12 You should stop playing football.	A doctor treating my hamstring injury.
13 Don't come back to see me if you don't take the medication.	A hospital consultant annoyed that I hadn't taken the medication he'd prescribed because I was anxious about the possible side effects.
14 Did you think you were going to talk and I was going to listen?	A counsellor I had gone to see about my anxiety and depression.

The utterances are as accurate as possible paraphrases, given many of them were said many years ago. Maybe I'm being too sensitive in my reactions and I'm misinterpreting what the doctors intended. But then that's a state that many patients find themselves in.

Here are some of the things that doctors have done to me over the years which have disturbed me:

- Performed a prostate massage on me in front of young trainee female doctors without asking for permission.
- Ended a consultation whilst I was still asking questions.
- Prescribed the wrong medication with serious consequences for me.
- Told me off for not taking prescribed medications which I suspected were inappropriate.
- Made mistakes about my previous medical history without reading my notes properly.
- Ignored my attempts at social interaction.
- Ignored me when I entered their office.
- Treated me as though I was unintelligent.
- Raised their voice at me because I'm old and therefore presumably deaf.
- Told me that I'd just have to put up with it because I was old.
- Told me to stop worrying.
- Talked down to me as an inferior.
- Not listened to what I was saying.
- Immediately announced a faulty diagnosis without asking any questions.
- Interrupted me whenever I tried to speak.
- Attributed all my problems to anxiety.
- Treated me without respect.

I'm sorry, Mrs Miggin, I myself have a medical condition that's difficult to treat. It's called 'Consultantitis'

These are just a few of the many negative things doctors have done to me over the many years, things which now make me apprehensive whenever I have an appointment scheduled with a doctor and things which make me rejoice on those occasions when a doctor does listen to me and does treat me with respect. Of course, there have been positive appointments too and many doctors have been helpful to me. And maybe I'm not always the best of patients. I suffer from anxiety and tend to worry and ask a lot of questions. That must be time-consuming and irritating for a lot of doctors

Here are some of the things I wish doctors would say to me more often:

- Good morning Mr Tomlinson (or even Brian as one doctor did actually address me recently). How are things with you?
- How was Chile?
- Did you manage to get your vaccination before you went to the conference in Jakarta?

- I've got some good news for you.
- Tell me all about it. Take your time.
- Is there anything else you'd like to tell me?
- This is what I think the problem could be.
- These are the options. You could … or … or you could… if you wanted to …
- Did you manage to finish that book you were telling me about?
- How about the pain you were getting in the knee? You haven't mentioned it.
- Goodbye, Mr Tomlinson. I hope things go well for you.

Some Suggestions Which Might Help

I understand that most doctors are working long hours, have long queues of patients waiting to see them, have another hospital or practice to go to, have committees to sit on, have conferences and training courses to attend and never have enough time to give to their patients. Like everybody else they are often tired, sometimes feel unwell and sometimes take problems with them to work. They are human beings, after all, and not just doctors. As patients, we need to be understanding and empathetic. But we are human beings too and not just patients, so doctors also need to be understanding and empathetic.

Here are some suggestions which might help doctors to become better and patients to become better. If nothing else is achieved, at least I'll feel better for making them.

Ideally doctors, like Dr Barr, should always wait for their patients to stop talking. But this obviously isn't realistic. There are other patients waiting to be seen and many other things to do. What I think is realistic, though, is for doctors to be encouraged to:

- Read the patients' recent notes **before** calling them in.
- Greet the patient with a smile.
- Use the patient's name at the beginning of the conversation.
- Have a brief chat to achieve human contact before focusing on the patient's problem.

- Invite the patient to tell them why they've come and to listen carefully to what they say.
- Ask a clarification question rather than make an interruption if the patient starts rambling and looks as though they might take too long.
- Examine the patient if relevant (even if a conclusion has been reached) to reassure them that a careful diagnosis is being made.
- Not announce a diagnosis until every possibility has been considered.
- Tell the patient their diagnosis and make sure they understand.
- Tell the patient what medication (if any) is being prescribed, give clear instructions on how to take it and point out (without alarming the patient) any side effects which are common in their experience.
- Ask the patient if they want to ask any further questions.
- End the conversation pleasantly and wish the patient well.

Throughout the appointment, it would really help the patient if they felt:

- As though they were having a conversation rather than being interrogated.
- At ease and comfortable.
- As though the doctor cared.
- They were being given time to explain their problem and ask questions about it.
- They were being listened to.

Conclusion

Here's a doctor patient dialogue:

Doctor: You're very sick.

Patient: Can I get a second opinion?

Doctor: Yes, of course! It's because you're fat.

Fortunately, the reality isn't quite as bad as that, but it does capture the frequent reality of the doctor being in charge, of the doctor initiating and closing the conversation and of the doctor not really responding to the patient's concern. Let's hope that doctor development courses, patient initiatives and increasing doctor self-awareness can change the situation and lead to the following type of conversation becoming the norm.

Doctor: Good morning, Mr Tomlinson. Or can I call you Brian?

Patient: Good morning, Dr Jones. Please do.

Doctor: And I'm Ivor.

Patient: From Wales?

Doctor: How did you guess? Yes, from Abergavenny.

Patient: I once spent the night there sleeping in a bus in the bus station.

Doctor: Can I ask why?

Patient: A kind Welsh policeman suggested it and a kind Welsh bus driver gave us a cup of tea.

Doctor (smiling): And how are things today?

Patient: Not too bad today. But then that always happens when I go to the doctor.

Doctor: That's what many patients tell me.

Patient: But I've been having a lot of pain recently in the groin.

Doctor: Tell me more. When does the pain come on? How long does it last?

Patient: Usually when I'm sitting down, especially at a table when I'm eating at home or in a restaurant. It can then last for a couple of hours, but it helps if I walk around a bit.

Doctor: I think I saw you in Wreckfish last week. There was a guy at the next table who suddenly shouted in pain and then got up and walked up and down.

Patient: That must have been me.

Doctor: I would have helped, but you seemed to recover and you seemed to be enjoying your meal.

Patient: Yeah. The pain wasn't too bad that time. And the wine helped. Sometimes though I have to stop my car, scream and then walk up and down for a long time.

Doctor: I'm going to send you to see a hip specialist. I know the pain's not in your hip, but pain in the groin can be a symptom of arthritis in the hip.

Patient: Is it OK if I take the dog for a walk?

Doctor: Yes, certainly. Exercise can help. But not too far.

Patient: How about the game tomorrow? Is it OK for me to go?

Doctor: Definitely. It'll take your mind off things. Well, it will if we win.

Patient: How long will I have to wait for an appointment?

Doctor: I'll mark it as urgent, but it could still be a couple of months. I'm prescribing some pain killers in case it becomes unbearable and maybe a glass of wine might help occasionally. Come back and see me if it gets a lot worse.

Oh… and enjoy the game tomorrow.

Patient: Thanks Doctor, I mean Ivor. Thanks for the chat.

Since writing the make-believe dialogue above I've actually had a conversation like it. It was with a doctor I've never met and was part of a telephone consultation. She actually started the conversation by saying, 'Hello, Brian,' and then chatted away throughout the consultation as though we were friends. She listened patiently, she answered all my questions with useful information, she didn't talk down to me, she was positive and supportive throughout, and she even laughed at some of my jokes. Afterwards, I felt so much better than before and really hoped that she would be seeing me the next time I visited the hospital. Unfortunately, that was not to be.

If you're a doctor reading this chapter, I hope you don't feel insulted and you do feel determined to be even more understanding, patient, empathetic and supportive than you are now. If you're a patient reading this, I hope that you'll be more understanding of the dilemma in which doctors find themselves and that you'll help them by preparing what you're going to say beforehand, by writing down your questions in advance, by keeping what you say as concise and informative as possible and by being pleasant and sociable. I also hope that more and more doctor patient interactions become social occasions, as well as effective medical transactions.

Finally, let me end on a positive note by saying that I've had two very positive interactions with doctors recently. One of the doctors greeted me with a sympathetic smile, listened carefully to what I had to say and then delivered the expected news that there wasn't anything they could do about it at the moment and I'd just have to learn to live with it. What's so positive about that? It was the sympathetic way he told me the truth. You could tell he really wanted to give me positive news, but respected me with the not-so-good news. He smiled sympathetically as I left and I did actually feel better than when I went in. The other doctor gave me good news, had a chat about shared interests we'd discovered during our previous meeting and reassured me that, if I was ever worried about my condition, I could just ring his secretary and he'd find a way of fitting me in for an appointment. Again, I felt better after the appointment than before it.

I must go and prepare for my doctor's appointment tomorrow. And maybe I'll have a beer to help me relax.

CHAPTER EIGHT

FROM THE HORSE'S MOUTH – CONFESSIONS OF A PHARMACIST

I am a pharmacist who dislikes taking medication. I wouldn't take decongestants for a runny nose from a cold or paracetamol for temperatures or headache. I mention these examples because a cold was the only thing I ever really had wrong with me until I was diagnosed with incurable cancer in my forties. Once I commenced treatment for cancer, I took my anti-cancer medication exactly as prescribed, I understood the importance of the treatment and the side effects were a risk worth taking. But I have told the doctor that I don't take some of the other medication they have prescribed for me. For example, I didn't take the anti-sickness medicines which made me drowsy or the chewable calcium tablets which made me feel sick.

Some background facts

In 2009, the National Institute for Clinical Excellence estimated that 1/3 to 1/2 of medicines prescribed for long-term conditions are not taken as recommended[234]. We know that medicine wastage is a huge problem—in 2009, a group appointed by the Department of Health estimated that we waste around £300 million of medicines each year, £150 million of which is avoidable[235]

This won't come as a surprise to anyone who has seen the piles of medicines brought into hospital by patients or their family members. Nor will it surprise healthcare professionals who visit patients'

---

[234] https://www.nice.org.uk/guidance/cg76/chapter/Introduction, accessed 10/06/2022

[235] https://discovery.ucl.ac.uk/id/eprint/1350234/1/Evaluation_of_NHS_ Medicines_Waste__web_publication_version.pdf, accessed 10/06/2022

homes to provide care. What came as a surprise to me is how easy it is to accumulate unwanted medicines when treatment changes or simply doesn't suit. We tend to supply medicine in large quantities to reduce repeat prescribing and because of pack sizes. Medicines wastage is an inevitable consequence. It's not just a waste of time and money, but also a safety concern. The quantity of wasted medication caused by patients not taking their medicines as prescribed would be reduced if healthcare professionals were to interact more effectively with patients.

What I learned as a trainee hospital pharmacist; the good, the bad and the ugly…

Before my cancer diagnosis, I was a healthy health care professional looking after 'the sick'. During my pharmacy training, I learned about the old fashioned 'health care practitioner knows best' approach to medicine, but also other, more patient-centred approaches. I now have experience of how it feels to be one of 'the sick' on the receiving end of some different practices.

As a trainee hospital pharmacist on a ward round, I found some of the doctors intimidating. I learned that often there are good reasons for the decisions made by a doctor or prescriber, but I also learned that sometimes they get it wrong. Every pharmacist will be able to tell you of one or two situations where they have intervened to correct a significant mistake by a prescriber.

One of the senior pharmacists where I trained was also quite intimidating, but he gave advice which I have never forgotten. He had trained as a pharmacist after a spell in hospital as a child with diabetes. His insider view into the life of a patient affected his practice and he influenced my approach because his advice was so effective. It was simply to speak to the patient about their medication and find out their thoughts. Explain what the reasons were for the prescriber choosing certain medication. The ridiculous thing is that this doesn't always happen when a patient is in hospital. Recommendations and changes to medication are sometimes made by healthcare professionals without anyone informing the patient of the decision.

Another piece of advice given to me by an experienced consultant colleague was that 'the patient is always right unless proven otherwise'.

That this needs to be stated is revealing. It can be simpler and more convenient to assume a patient is a clueless idiot with mistaken beliefs which need to be corrected. Stories of patients spraying inhalers onto their chests or swallowing the desiccant from the box of tablets form part of the folklore of Pharmacy. These tales illustrate only that some patients have not had clear enough information and not that they are inherently incompetent or have questionable motives. As health care professionals, we see many examples of patients misunderstanding instructions or becoming confused about their treatment.

Speaking for myself as a patient, there have been more than a few occasions where I feel like a healthcare professional has spoken to me and treated me as if I am stupid. My reaction to this behaviour does not make me feel inclined to accept any advice that this healthcare professional may offer.

I didn't agree with the advice which I used to give when it was given to me

I used to be a health care professional who urged people to take their anti-sickness medication regularly as it works best to prevent, rather than relieve, nausea. One of the routine questions that the chemotherapy nurses ask patients is 'have you had any nausea or vomiting?' because this is often a side effect of the treatment. In my case, however, as a result of my cancer progression, I had started vomiting on a fairly regular basis at roughly the same time of day. I didn't feel nauseous, it did not affect my appetite and my observations were that the anti-sickness medicines I was prescribed were not effective in stopping me vomiting. Additionally, I didn't like the side effects of drowsiness that the anti-sickness medicines gave me. I think that the chemotherapy nurse felt like she *should* offer a solution to the problem, which was to advise me to take the anti-sickness medication regularly. The solution didn't involve asking me why I didn't want to take the anti-sickness medicines, so I ignored her advice and felt a little irritated by it. With the help of one of the doctors, I later found an approach which worked better for me using a different anti sickness medication and timing.

I accepted a prescription for tablets which I didn't think would help me

The tablets were to ease a cramping pain I had experienced, and the doctor suggested I try them. I told her I was reluctant as I had never observed these tablets to be especially effective when taken by patients. I agreed to try the tablets, but I was supplied with three boxes of 56 tablets. I have taken perhaps five tablets and my conclusion is they didn't really help, but the problem seems to have gone away in any case. Perhaps the tablets could have been useful, but I wish they hadn't issued me with such a large quantity. Maybe I will require the tablets one day, but I now have further boxes added to my collection of medicines at home. Quantity of tablets supplied is one of the requirements for writing a prescription, but not enough thought always goes into what amount is really needed.

Reflecting on my experiences with unheeded advice and unwanted tablets:

> *I wonder if healthcare professionals sometimes feel they ought to offer a treatment which patients feel they ought to accept, despite both parties suspecting it's not a good idea?*

Repeated blood tests and visits to hospital are no fun for patients

I had been taking the first line treatment for my cancer for about two years when some tests started to concern the oncologist that the cancer was becoming resistant to treatment. He requested a scan which backed up his suspicion. When I attended clinic to get my scan results, it seemed to me that the oncologist only looked at the scan results once I was in the room for my appointment. During the appointment, he offered me a couple of treatment options—a clinical trial or another slightly more established treatment. I was to decide before my next appointment in one week and, in the meantime, he put the next cycle of my current treatment on hold. By the time of my next appointment, the oncologist had found out that I wouldn't be eligible for the trial. After discussing with a colleague, he recommended a different approach of continuing my current treatment until I could qualify for the trial and then deciding.

After the second appointment with the oncologist, I attended my next treatment appointment in the expectation that nothing was changing with my medicines. As usual, I went to the blood clinic as soon as they opened on the morning of my appointment. When I got to the treatment centre, I found that my prescription had not been restarted after being put on hold. I asked the nurse to confirm that this was correct, and she found out that this was an oversight and the doctor had meant to continue the treatment. However, it hadn't been ordered from the pharmacy and apparently it would take two days to resolve the issue. I was asked to come back tomorrow for another blood test as the one I'd had today wouldn't be valid in two days' time. I was also told that I should attend the following day to pick up the prescription.

This wasn't a good solution for me. I was still working as a pharmacist, and this would mean taking time off work for more appointments. Also, I have had a few bad experiences with people taking blood, so I am not keen to have any more blood tests than necessary. I asked the nurse if I could speak to the pharmacist to explain my situation. The pharmacist didn't come to speak to me, but, after a short delay, I was told that she now said that my prescription could be ready the next day, meaning I didn't need a further blood test.

From the perspective of the pharmacist and nurse, they undoubtedly had a lot of work to process. The prescription hadn't been written and they were sorting out someone else's oversight. It was just another situation where someone had been busy and forgotten to do something. I am grateful that they listened to my side of the story and came up with a better solution, but equally:

I am aware that not all patients would question the initial approach.

Doctor: Ms Johnson I'm going to prescribe neurosurgery.
Patient: Er....for ingrowing toenails doctor?

What a better approach would have been for me as a patient

If the doctor had checked what options were available to me before I went into my appointment, the whole misunderstanding with the cancelled prescription would then never have happened. The oncologist would have avoided needing to see me a second time and I would have avoided another hospital visit.

The nurse and pharmacist were left to resolve the problem. They were undoubtedly familiar with having to pick up the pieces, and this is often a thankless task. But, as I patient, I only want a solution which works for me. I would prefer to minimise my time coming to and from hospital. Also, I'd like healthcare staff to remember that getting blood tests is not a pleasant experience for patients and trips to and from hospital take a considerable time. I don't want my days to be planned around appointments, but I can see how easily this could happen.

I am in a relatively privileged position compared to many patients. I make sure I fully understand my treatment and what the medical team are telling me. If there is something I don't understand, I will ask for clarification. I know where and when to attend my many blood tests, appointments and scans. I know what medication I should be prescribed and if it has been omitted. I know to confirm things, because I also know that things don't always get remembered. My career as a pharmacist has involved asking questions and checking that no mistakes have been made. I don't ask for special treatment, but:

> *not all patients have these advantages. They may be too respectful of the team to ask questions; they may not be able to read appointment letters or understand written or spoken information given to them.*

A hospital can be an intimidating environment for a patient

In 2020, after shielding from coronavirus for 6 months, I was invited to an appointment to see a specialist in the hospital. Staff were walking around the corridors not always wearing masks correctly and patients for the clinic were told to join a queue in the corridor. On entering the clinic, a healthcare assistant asked me to remove my mask so she could check my temperature by placing a thermometer under my tongue. I found this extremely alarming in view of the way that the COVID-19 virus is transmitted. Another type of thermometer could have been used, preferably a forehead scanner. Once I had had my temperature checked, the receptionist asked me to remove my mask again as she couldn't understand what I was saying with the mask on. When I got into the room to see the specialist, he expressed surprise that I had not been offered a telephone appointment. I reported how anxious this whole experience had made me feel by contacting the patient advice and liaison service (PALS). The clinic manager telephoned me the same day and agreed that this situation was unacceptable and was putting clinically vulnerable patients at risk. She would use my example to change practice.

How many other patients just accepted this situation because they were being instructed in what to do by hospital staff in a hospital setting?

My advice to patients

Be friendly and respectful to all staff, from the cleaner to the consultant, but if something doesn't seem right, ask questions. If you're really not happy about something and don't know who to speak to use the hospital PALS service.

Tell the prescriber if you can't tolerate a medicine because there is usually a good alternative.

If a choice doesn't seem right, it is always worth asking why. Often there is a good reason for a choice and, if this is the case, the prescriber or a member of the team can explain their thinking, but occasionally mistakes are made.

I am sorry to report that some health service staff need to work on the way they present information and interact with patients. That's why we ask for feedback, and I encourage you to give this feedback. I hope you will also experience many really helpful and beneficial interactions with healthcare professionals.

*Take three of these Mr Bloggs every other day unless there's an 'r' in the month
and it's 9 days after a bank holiday or Liverpool are playing at home
and the moon is in its third quarter....*

Please let the pharmacist know about that pile of unwanted and possibly out-of-date medication that you have at home! The pharmacist will ensure that it is disposed of safely.

My advice to health professionals… including pharmacists

Time saved by not listening will mean your interaction with the patient could be entirely wasted.

It's convenient to revert to a 'speaking to the patient' manner, imparting knowledge and giving instructions. Sometimes this is necessary, but acting in this robotic manner is likely to be counterproductive.

Really listening to what the patient is telling you is a difficult task.

The patient may think you are clever and nice, but did you find out what their real concern and understanding was?

Are you offering a solution in the form of advice or a prescription without understanding what the problem is?

Is this saving you time, or does it mean that you or someone else needs to spend more time at some point in the future?

'Just' listening...

Things which have helped me

I imagined that I would need to come to terms with my diagnosis of having a terminal illness, with the knowledge that my health will deteriorate and my life expectancy has been reduced by at least 30 years. The future which I had imagined was not going to happen. How can I learn to accept my new future? One of my friends advised seeking distractions and this has worked well for me. Riding my mountain bike, meeting friends, going for walks, doing (easy) crosswords, taking an interest in nature, feeling pleased to see a greenfinch eating from the bird feeder I had filled the day before. I realise now that these distractions aren't really distractions at all, but are activities which bring me joy. I try to notice the things I enjoy and to plan my days, so they centre around these things, not appointments or discussions about illness.

Concluding thoughts

I can't continue to do my job as a pharmacist, but I would like other healthcare professionals to reflect and learn from my observations.

I don't think the 'NHS heroes' narrative is helpful for patients as it perpetuates the idea that the healthcare professionals are godlike figures and not to be questioned. I would, therefore, like other patients to remember that healthcare professionals need to listen to you, and you should ask for explanations.

CHAPTER NINE

FROM THE HORSE'S MOUTH –
A *SECOND* DOCTOR'S OPINION
(AKA A SOLUTION FOCUS JUST *WORKS*
ACROSS ALL OF MEDICINE)

A very quick intro[236]: I'm Sharryn—sometimes Dr Sharryn. Paediatric Emergency Medicine is my specialty and is the best job in the world... really, it is, and nobody could convince me otherwise! So, while this is different to oncology, exactly the same principles apply.

Working with the whole family and the whole story...

I work with families, rather than exclusively children, and often my work is with the parent or grandparent. That's good—it's the families and those interactions rather than the medicine that 'make' my job. Parents are often much more anxious or upset about their child's health than they might be about their own. They often feel helpless or overwhelmed or have ongoing challenges or exhaustion.

They have whole complicated lives outside the tiny sliver of their lives that I see. I need to be able to communicate with all of them 'where they are'. That's a lot of the skill in my role as the Consultant

---

[236] I've never been into those long bios. Most of the families I see don't know my surname, and say they saw the lovely Scottish (or Irish) doctor with the reddish hair. That's usually specific enough to identify me! I'm a Consultant Paediatrician—many other Healthcare staff say they just couldn't do Paediatrics—all those heart-breaking, sick children. And the parents... Heck, I only did Paediatric Surgery as my first job just to get over the fear of children. I did get over the fear and also got hooked!

and that's where Solution Focus shines. A lot of my communication is actually with adults (70% of our patients are under five and large numbers under one).

I also see parents or carers in a separate clinic as 'the patient' often after a Child's A&E visit when they are struggling either with coping with the child or their symptoms, or with health anxiety or fear. My manager[237] might argue that they don't pay me to do that. This is fair—on the surface. Actually, however, working with the family *does*, in fact, treat the child.

A powerful alternative to the 'Medical Model'

In a normal medical practice, a doctor will often make some (sensible) assumptions from any initial information and drive the consultation to tease out important supporting (and refuting) information to reach a diagnosis and then plan any treatment. The patient will often have that feeling of being steered through a planned series of questions and may feel that they had little opportunity to direct the consultation.

Solution-Focused (SF) conversations don't often even start with what might be seen as the issue.

That's pretty ground-breaking!

They start with what matters to somebody, right here, right now. I have no role in directing that conversation, save asking good enough questions to keep eliciting good, rich information. I don't need to know the underlying issues and they are likely not directly related to any 'solutions' anyway. That's not to say I'm not interested—of course I am, and I am compassionate (rather than sympathetic or merely empathic) in hearing about them. The 'not knowing' answer allows a lot of freedom. You do need to really concentrate, though, to properly listen to that answer, as well as formulate a good next

---

[237] Spoiler alert: there are lots of things I do that my managers might not see as my job and are just the right thing to do.

question. Notice that it's not 'the' next good question. There will often be a whole lot of directions or approaches that we could take.

You would think that this wouldn't work in A&E—it's too urgent, too fast.

This isn't actually the case. We see children (with their families):

- Who self-harm or feel suicidal. They are often so scared and ashamed when they come and feel a burden. When the first clinician they see really listens and pushes them to think what they are hoping for, this sets things up nicely to meet the CAMHS team the next day with hope. They also bring adults who are often distraught and feel angry and helpless.
- With 'functional' abdominal pain. I hate that term—it sort of means it's only in their heads. It sort of is. Your gut drives your brain, and your brain drives your gut—it's not called the gut-brain axis for nothing. How could it be stopped? They also bring adults with them looking for answers and cures and whose day-to-day lives are ruled (and ruined) by these symptoms.
- With migraines, which cause stress and then lead to more migraines; conversations about what works and what matters to them help that whole cycle. They bring adults with them who wish they could take on their child's stress and pain.
- With anxiety in its purest form; sadly, generalised anxiety is increasingly common. Symptoms like panic attacks, headaches, reflux and gastritis (acid reflux or acid stomach) are often driven by anxiety. We never saw this when I qualified now a sizeable minority have it. Medication can temporarily mask symptoms, but only treating the stress, anxiety or depression actually 'cures' it. These children bring with them adults who hate to see their anxiety build to a point where it's out of control.
- Who might have been off school and can't manage going back. Their parents just don't know what to do to help.
- With long-COVID and ME. Their parents want answers and treatment options—not just time.

- With severe anger who have injured themselves (or others). Their families may have been physically assaulted and will almost always have been really scared and hurt by their words. They and their parents often just can't cope and have nowhere else to go. Their families are often desperate and have no one offering to help.
- Who others might describe as neurodiverse who are struggling with tics or other issues. Their parents expected challenges and they might have seen their child dismissed.
- With gender identity or orientation worries. Their families may be supportive or not. Either way, they know that their child is suffering and may have no idea how to start to help.

In every healthcare setting, the nurses know exactly what is going on and exactly the strengths (and weaknesses) of the doctors they work with. They don't even have to be in the room—they see patients as they come in and go out and that tells the biggest story. They hear patients talking as they leave. They just know! So, it's no surprise that the nurses quickly picked up that this worked with our most demanding families and patients with the most intractable problems, as well as those with mental health challenges (where previously we would just attempt to refer to our mental health services CAMHS).

A larger and larger proportion of patient notes are now slipped into my hand as 'this looks like a good one for you'.

A full session can take an hour. But 10 minutes can have a huge impact.[238]

---

[238] Often it's just a Pattern Interrupt, which is when something really unexpected happens which then makes us instantly more open to what happens straight after it. That's also a hypnotherapy technique interestingly— the pattern interrupt is so unexpected that it temporarily opens the mind. We need to use that period of openness to good effect.

More tales from the sharp end (1): SF in the Resus Room

Most children were well before they came and will be well when they leave. Some are much sicker or have underlying illnesses and this is harder emotionally. Some are critically ill. It might seem odd to relish these big resuscitations (while not wanting any child to ever need resuscitation), as well as being heavily invested in Solution Focus work. I honestly think that these work well together.

One often-cited criticism of the Solution-Focused Approach is that it looks too woolly. It takes too much time.

This isn't actually the case. *I am often the one leading critical resuscitations*. I hate generally being the centre of attention, and especially cringe at much praise. I do know deep down that, when anything might be hitting the fan, I'm one of the folks that the team want to be there.

Solution Focus can cut through in these situations.

My most memorable times are of some of the sickest children. Sometimes it is connecting with families and talking about their child at a cardiac arrest. Sometimes it's avoiding any medical talk at all and using phrases like 'you've cared for him so much', 'do you think he's trying to tell us something?', 'it must be so tough fighting this again and again' that allow honest and frank discussions. Giving purely medical explanations at these times often feels like hiding behind the medical facts.

More tales from the sharp end (2): SF and Complaints

Strangely, one of my most enjoyable parts of the job is dealing with complaints. Thankfully, we get very few!

As Dominic says, we almost need to reach the low of getting it all out there before we can make progress. I do this by asking a few polite questions after we have chatted a little about them. If that doesn't bring the issues out (and often you feel the underlying anger), I throw in a proverbial grenade - 'there was a little issue with', 'somebody slightly missed X…'. It allows them to start by correcting this perceived slight and then really let rip. I encourage that letting rip.

I notice other doctors aren't always comfortable with that[239].

Few people can rant for more than 2 minutes, though it might often seem longer. Once the rage dies down, the nuggets of what to work with start to emerge.

Part of why this works is that I have one of those faces that is incapable of hiding anything (even, as it turns out, in a mask!). People see how shocked and sympathetic I am.

This provides a chance to give people a *good listening to* and then a chance to go above and beyond to get things right. Many of my favourite families[240] I first met after a complaint.

The art of medicine—concerted listening

One should meet people where they are, then ask some questions. More important than asking questions is really listening to the answers—and giving time when an answer isn't immediately forthcoming. Dominic loves to use Zippy[241] as a prompt to remember to zip it and listen! Female clinicians do seem to allow more time.

Silence is very powerful. Most people find silence uncomfortable and tend to open up[242]. I really had to learn to stop to allow patients and families to answer my questions, and so had to physically   sit back on my hands. I needed some very obvious and physical to mark the fact that I was doing this[243]. Ridiculous maybe, but it worked!

---

[239] 'aren't always' is doing some heavy lifting there!
[240] Much like Bruce Forsyth, really, they are *all* my favourites.
[241] A character in the ITV series *Rainbow*.
[242] However, if it goes on too long, it really causes discomfort and disrupts the relationship between the clinician and patient.
[243] Otherwise, I tend to lean forwards and talk quite quickly. Maintaining that dynamic was completely incompatible with any degree of silence.

Physicians heal thyselves...

In every healthcare setting, and in every specialty, there are patients or families perceived as 'too hard', 'non-compliant', or 'too demanding', for whom 'nothing can be done'. There are many great things about being a consultant, and, in the early days, seeing all of these was hard. It kept me awake at night. It wore me down so much that I had so little to really offer even when I dearly wished I could. Since I started using SF, I have found that there is a way forward. Things can be better.

My happy accident wasn't Penicillin—it was fairy dust.

I found SFT quite by accident. I worked with the best mental health nurse (ever) known as *CAMHS Clare*[244] who showed me that we really could do something for the exploding numbers of young people presenting with mental health issues or medical symptoms caused or exacerbated by mental health issues.

It's like a genie: once it's out, you can't put it back. Clare was very rightly promoted, and I knew I had to attempt to fill some of that new gap.

Solution-Focused Therapy training was found by a bit of (quite intensive) Googling. I wish I had known then that I lived in Southport - the near-epicentre of the SF world!

You didn't need to be a trained psychologist and a foundation course[245] took 4 days and also was relatively cheap.

One of my patients' mums described using the approach as like I'd sprinkled some fairy dust—she couldn't see how it worked as it was 'just' a conversation, but work it did! This was for medical problems that normally would have needed medications.

---

[244] Clare used a method that focused on strengths although not SF. She also just understood that medical symptoms were often driven or maintained or exacerbated by psychological factors.

[245] For example,   *https://www.brief.org.uk/courses*

Those 4 days changed my life!

That sounds just a bit dramatic, doesn't it? Put it into context though… I started medical training in 1988 and had had 20+ years of training and using the medical (pathology) model. That model was often spluttering and failing as time went on, and you can either try and battle on or look for something different. I was looking for something different as a bit of an aside, an add-on.

Solution Focus was a bit more dramatic than that—it literally turned everything on its head! It's *just not up to me* to magic a cure for all from my rabbit hat.

It just made so much sense. Some things that came out in the Solution-Focused training I already did, not knowing they contributed and then it completely changed much of my problem-focused work. Medicine is truly pathology-focused.

So, when I see colleagues in Paediatrics and all other specialties[246] being worn down by the sheer numbers where the Medical Model spluttered and stalled, I gently extol the virtues of Solution Focus work.

---

[246] Come on, you knew we all have lots of other doctor friends, right?

I'm noticing low mood, hopelessness, apathy...... but what are **your** *problems Ms Smith?*
I prescribe a quiet lie down doctor to clear your head so you can ask me what my plans
are and how I'm going to get there..

Surprisingly, it can be a hard sell—it's almost too good to be true!

Doctors are often scared as they are so invested in the Medical Model, and will still have to use it in part. SF doesn't cover the whole conversation, even if it drives the structure. But demonstrating that magic, sprinkling that fairy dust live[247] can be a strong driver to pursue it.

We pride ourselves on being rational scientists who objectively weigh evidence, so it would take a weight of real-life evidence as well as scientific papers to allow many doctors to take that leap.

It's not, by the way, that I believe for a moment that doctors completely rooted in the Medical Model don't care. Over a period of 30 years, I wouldn't need a whole hand to count the number of uncaring doctors I've worked with.

---

[247] Or, even better, on the doctor themselves as a recipient!

Many doctors go into medicine because they like people—and, of course, for the academic and intellectual challenges[248]. But it always comes back to the people.

Here are some things I was already doing before SF training:

- Going out into the waiting room and talking to families—just chatting about general things, not medical issues. I hadn't even noticed, but I had been building rapport before we even started.
- I often help carry coats or push pushchairs for mums weighed down with baby paraphernalia. I thought it was just helpful. It also shows 'I get how hard having young children is and I want to help. I respect you in trying to manage everything.'
- I usher patients into the space first[249]—this stops it being my space that they come into. They get first choice of where to sit (and children often take the doctor's swivel chair!).
- When patients came again what did I strive to remember, their blood test results or their amazing pyjamas? It's the 'what makes you, *you'* that has always been my 'bread and butter'.

Here are some things I've learned since:

- Despite all our medical training, despite all that studying and all that experience, increasingly *we just don't have the answers*[250].
- Further, we don't think patients can accept that sometimes we don't know the answer—spoiler alert: often patients respect us much more for being honest and for searching for an answer.

---

[248] And in my case, the thankfully rare huge adrenaline cases.

[249] Dominic and I once had a conversation about making the patient and family feel like the most important people in the world during the consultation and we called this the 'Terry Wogan Effect', after *the* Radio 2 Breakfast Show host for decades who managed to make every listener nationwide feel that it was a conversation just between them.

[250] Instead, we can develop a different expertise: asking the right questions at the right moment.

- Seeing us work through possibilities rather than throwing a label out there is also really useful. Patients don't see it as indecisive—they see it as caring to take the time to find an answer.
- Ringing up after an appointment because you thought of something else or just to check up on the patient goes down well. Doctors think it makes it look like they weren't up to the job at the first appointment or that it looks like they missed something. Patients often see it as really caring and seeing them as important enough to even think about.
- Being present and being honest really help patients. They want us there with them not distracted. So-called small talk makes us present with them and establishes that personal connection quickly.
- What I also love about working with children is that if you ask them if they have any questions, they can be brutal! They can also ask some really cool questions! If you ask what they think of any advice, they will tell you. And if you ask if advice might work for them, they will either tell you it will or won't. Healthcare planning is a two-way process: the patient's knowledge and fears and experience together with some of my experience, investigations and suggestions. We decide together.

It's almost as if all the things that we think make us look bad can often do the opposite.

Spreading the love **beyond** *paediatric medicine and what it takes*

Shouldn't there always be someone for all patients though? If more clinicians were able to embrace this SF way of working, we could achieve so much more. Most importantly, patients will get better— and much quicker. Regardless of any savings the NHS makes, the benefit of SF to the patient and society as a whole is a no-brainer. And the NHS will also make huge savings on frequent attenders who no longer need to come, as well as unnecessary medication costs.

If it was a stock market share, I'd be telling everyone I know to buy, buy, buy!

One of the real beauties of it is that is can apply in virtually any situation. It is in no way limited by the age of the patient and indeed they can be somebody you could encounter in any walk of life. I use this approach in many different situations—I've used it in a road rage situation, and in a restaurant when things went wrong.

This is far from a little something on the side for Paediatricians.

So, if it's just a conversation, it must be easy right?

Anything but! The technique can be taught quickly and understood quickly. What is hard is asking good questions ('good' in that they bring meaty answers from the patient).

Unlike a normal medical history, there is no question list. Each answer drives the next question.

Listening really hard and continuously coming up with good questions is really (really) hard!

In the past I had a huge armoury of medical treatments—they were all blunt and useless in the face of these issues.

It turns out that conversation is often the answer, not pills.

Knowing you have something to offer changes everything; you don't dread these patients and actively take them on. They'll often have had plenty of experience of being sidelined or avoided.

You, as a doctor, can break that pattern. You, by working as a co-expert with the patient, can help them completely change their lives.

Concluding Thoughts

Honestly, the week I went on that Solution-Focused Foundation course *I was close to burnout*. Like most clinicians, I just didn't know it.

Right now, hopefully heading towards the post-pandemic period,[251] many colleagues will be physically and mentally exhausted due to what they have experienced and for having to keep getting up and doing it all over again. There is limited provision for these caring individuals (or their families), and I fear that our health services will see many of them drift away from healthcare.

My own situation years before the pandemic was of trying and trying to find a way to help these patients where medicines had no answer, and I knew they needed psychological support. They kept coming back in hope and I'd exhausted all of my options. I felt that I was failing, when, in actual fact, I only needed a different perspective as much as new tools.

It was the turning of things on their head that allowed me to break free from the need to play the doctor and find the fix. The difference that the shedding that made was not just big, it was mahoosive!

Once that lifted, it stopped me ruminating on all the patients I couldn't help and dreaded coming back. It showed that I did not need to be perfect[252], but, instead, should be authentic and honest with families. It also allowed me to thrive again outside medicine as that constant burden had lifted.

It allowed me to become me again.

It also allowed me to pick up these formerly dreaded patients and feel confident that we could do good work together. Just being able to go in with positivity and confidence almost makes better outcomes inevitable on its own.

That's what families really crave. They know we're human.

It didn't affect how much I cared. In fact, if anything, I could care more because I wasn't so burdened with expectation. And most of all, outcomes are better and families are happier. I'm happier. I'm human and it's not selfish to want my life to be easier and happier—

---

[251] With literally everything crossed.

[252] I never was, and never would have been, perfect.

it makes me a better clinician. Some of my most treasured patients came from a complaints process. They cared enough to complain.

Doctors are often proudest of their medical prowess.

I'm proudest that the nurses steer those most in need to me and bring their own children to me.

Nothing beats positively impacting someone's life.

Saving lives is what people think we crave; in fairness, it takes some beating and I get to do it sometimes.

Seeing children after SF is rewarding *every single day*.

While learning SF, I have been used as a guinea pig and been cured of my crippling inability to be late. And I no longer have imposter syndrome[253].

Solution-Focused approaches have changed mine and my patients' lives.

Someday they will spread from the Southport epicentre and will take over the world.

That is my and Dominic's dream.

---

[253] Ok, everybody has a little!

CHAPTER TEN

THE USUAL END BITS

Proper Acknowledgements

In the end, and in keeping with the Solution-Focused principle of *not knowing*, most of the credit for the material is due to the patients and their families who have had the, er, pleasure of working with me over the years; for example, the one woman who said to me 'You should deal with every patient like they were the Queen'. She was exactly right. Thanks to all my colleagues over the years who've had the dubious joy of working with me. And the luminaries of Solution-Focused thinking over the years who freely share their best ideas; I'd like to think I've carried on this tradition. If you, in turn, go on to use any of my stuff, please acknowledge where it came from.

My grateful thanks to the very generous Dr Brian Tomlinson, Ms. Anne Waddington and Dr Sharryn Gardner, authors of Chapters 7, 8 and 9, and for Professors Deborah Christie and May Ng who commented on an earlier version of this tome—the cheque's in the post folks. Well, sort of. Similarly, Ms. Rebecca Gladders from Cambridge Scholars Publishing, who, unprompted, very kindly and patiently proofread my scribblings…. the world needs more people like you!

Ultimately, at the risk of going all 'Hollywood', all (if there are any) royalties go to charity and I thank God, for, ultimately, everything. Yes, really.

And, finally, I'd like to thank my family especially my wife for spending my salary… and… supporting me for, well, ever. But no thanks to our delinquent dog Millie.

Predictable Disclaimers

Although I'm NHS through and through like the letters in a stick of rock, my pronouncements may, or may not, reflect the views, policies, etc., of my NHS Trust (hopefully they do). Also, I've done my best to get my sourcing right but plead for forgiveness for any errors. Finally, I've anonymised names and stories to maintain confidentiality; some patients I have met over the years may recognise bits of themselves in there; if they do, I hope they feel I've got it right!

BIBLIOGRAPHY/RESOURCES

Chapter 1

Buscaglia, L (1924-1998) *Please Listen* (abridged).

Bray, D. (2020) *Unleashing the Solution-Focused Power of the Ormskirk Model by Minding Your Language* Diabetes Care for Children & Young People 10 (1) p.58. (https://diabetesonthenet.com/diabetes-care-children-young-people/unleashing-the-solution-focused-power-of-the-ormskirk-model-by-minding-your-language/)

Clover, B (2020) *Urgent cancer treatment down 60 per cent in April.* Health Service Journal, June 2020.

Coifman, K.G., Flynn, J.J. & Pinto, L.A. (2016) *When context matters: Negative emotions predict psychological health and adjustment.* Motiv Emot 40, 602–624.

Fox, E. (1997) *Predominance of the Curative Model of Medical Care: A Residual Problem.* JAMA. 278(9) 761-763.

Health Foundation (2012) https://www.health.org.uk/publications/when-doctors-and-patients-talk-making-sense-of-the-consultation.

Kubler-Ross, E (2008). *On Death and Dying.* Abingdon: Routledge.

Lee, F. (2005) *If Disney Ran Your Hospital: 9 1/2 Things You Would Do Differently* (2005). Second River Healthcare Press: Bozeman.

Murray, J (2010, accessed 10/06/2022) (https://www.dailymail.co.uk/health/article-1247850/Positive-thinking-makes-sick-JENNI-MURRAY-hates-self-help-industry.html#ixzz4am4rCZac

Nouwen, H.J.M., (1981) *The Way of the Heart: Desert Spirituality and Contemporary Ministry* p. 34. New York: Seabury Press

Rosenberg, M.B. *Nonviolent Communication: A Language of Life*, 3rd edition (2015) Encinitas (USA): Puddledancer Press, p. 3

University of Queensland (2014, accessed 10/06/2022) *A positive boost to the immune system* [Psychoneuroimmunology]

https://www.uq.edu.au/news/article/2014/09/positive-boost-immune-system

Youngson, R (2012) *Time to Care*. Raglan (NZ): Rebelheart

Chapter 2

Curda, A. (2011). *The Damocles Syndrome: Where We Are Today*. J Canc Educ 26, 397–398.

Meatloaf & Steinman, J. (1977) *All Revved Up with No Place to Go*. Lyrics © 1977 Round Hill Music Big Loud Songs, Carlin America Inc. from the album Bat out of Hell.

Nolen, J.L. (accessed 10/06/2022) *Mnemonic*. https://www.britannica.com/topic/mnemonic.

Perry, J. & Croft, D. (1968-1977) *Dad's Army*. BBC TV/Radio Series.

van Osch, M. et al. (2014, accessed 10/06/2022) *Reducing patients' anxiety and uncertainty, and improving recall in bad news consultations*. Health Psychology, 33(11), 1382–1390. https://doi.org/10.1037/hea0000097.

Vicianova, M (2015) *Historical Techniques of Lie Detection*, Eur J Psychol. Aug; 11(3): 522–534.

Chapter 3

Berg, I. K. (1989). *Of visitors, complainants, and customers: Is there really such a thing as "resistance?'* Family Therapy Networker, 13(1): 21.

Bray, D. et al. (2015) *'First, do no harm': a solution-focused approach to pain measurement and management.* European Journal of Palliative Care 22(4) 190-193.

Brainyquote. https://www.brainyquote.com/topics/deathbed-quotes.

Chisholm, T. (1866–1960) *Great Is Thy Faithfulness*. Pub. 1923 by Hope Publishing Carol Stream: IL

Dexter, C. & Warren, T. (1987 onwards) *Inspector Morse* (and sequels). ITV Studios.

Geller, B. (1966 – 1973) *Mission: Impossible*. CBS Television.

Hoyt, M. (1996) *A Golfer's Guide to Brief Therapy* in Constructive Therapies 2. Guildford Press.

NHS (accessed 10/06/2022). *End of life care.*
https://www.nhs.uk/conditions/end-of-life-
care/?tabname=planning-ahead

O'Hanlon, B and Beadle, S. (2000) *A Field Guide to Possibility Land.*
BT Press: London.

Smith, M. L., Glass, G. V., & Miller, T. I. (1980). *The benefits of psychotherapy.* Baltimore, MD: John Hopkins University Press.

Spice Girls (1996) - *Wannabe.* © Sony/ATV Music Publishing LLC,
Universal Music Publishing Group, Peermusic Publishing.

Thomas, D. (1954) *Under Milk Wood.* BBC Radio Production.

Yeats, W.B. (1865-1939): *The Cloths of Heaven.* in, for example,
The Collected Poems of W.B. Yeats (1996) ed. Richard Finneran.
Scribner: NYC.

Chapter 4

Bunyan, J. (1678). *The Pilgrim's Progress.* Multiple publishers.

Sansom, C. J. (2003 onwards). The *Shardlake* series. Macmillan:
NYC.

Chapter 5

Awdish, R. (2018) *In Shock: how nearly dying made me a better intensive care doctor.* Bantam Press: London.

Brief: The Centre for Solution Focused Practice. (accessed
10/06/2022). https://www.brief.org.uk/

Bon Jovi, J. (1994) *Someday I'll Be Saturday Night* from the album
Cross Road: the Best of Bon Jovi. © Mercury

Breast Cancer Now (UK-based, accessed 10/06/2022)
https://breastcancernow.org.

Cheshire and Merseyside Cancer Alliance (UK-based, accessed
10/06/2022). https://www.cmcanceralliance.nhs.uk

Department of Health. (2001, UK-based, accessed 10/06/2022) *The
expert patient: a new approach to chronic disease management
for the twenty-first century.* London: Department of Health.
https://webarchive.nationalarchives.gov.uk/+/http://www.dh.gov
.uk/en/Publicationsandstatistics/Publications/PublicationsPolicy
AndGuidance/DH_4006801.

Donne, J. (1572-1631) *Devotions Upon Emergent Occasions, and severall steps in my Sicknes*, - Meditation XVII, 1624.

Giono, J. (1954) *The Man who Planted Trees*. Harvill Press: London. https://www.penguin.co.uk/books/105/1052261/the-man-who-planted-trees/9781860461170.html,

Kingsley, E.P. (1987, accessed 10/06/2022) *Welcome to Holland* https://www.emilyperlkingsley.com/welcome-to-holland

Macmillan UK (accessed 10/06/2022) https://www.macmillan.org.uk

Minghella, D. et al. (2004-2019). *Doc Martin* ITV Studios.

Nixon, R. (1913-1994). *Only if you have been in the deepest valley, can you ever know how magnificent it is to be on the highest mountain.* https://www.brainyquote.com/quotes/richard_m_nixon_159252 accessed 10/06/2022.

Paul of Tarsus (c. 05 – c. 64/65 AD) Philippians 4:11-14.

Prostate Cancer UK (accessed 10/06/2022 https://prostatecanceruk.org/ https://prostatecanceruk.org

Straube, P. (2011, accessed 10/06/2022) *The Starfish Story: one step towards changing the world.* The original story is by Loren Eiseley (1907–1977) in The Star Thrower, pub. 1978, Random House: New York, but it has many versions. This one is at https://eventsforchange.wordpress.com/2011/06/05/the-starfish-story-one-step-towards-changing-the-world.

Unwin, D. & Unwin, J. *The Grin Model.* https://bhma.org/wp-content/uploads/2019/06/GRIN-Unwins-JHH-16.2.pdf, reproduced with authors' permission.

Working Conversations (UK-based, accessed 10/06/2022) https://workingconversationsgroup.org/lets-keep-talking

Chapter 6

Alinsky, S.D. (2010) *Rules for Radicals* (reissue ed). London: Vintage.

Bannink, F. (2012) *Practicing Positive CBT: From Reducing Distress to Building Success* Chichester: Wiley-Blackwell.

Berkeley, G. (1685- 1753); e.g. N. Warburton (2011), *A Little History of Philosophy*. Yale University Press, p87.

Blayney, S (2014) *Survival as medical registrar on call: remember the doughnut.* Clinical Medicine, Vol 14, No 5: 506–9

Bliss, E. and Bray, D. *The smallest solution focused particles.* Journal of Systemic Therapies 28 (2) 62-74.

Bray, D. et al. (2015) *'First, do no harm': a solution-focused approach to pain measurement and management.* European Journal of Palliative Care. 22(4) 190-193.

British Tinnitus Association (accessed 10/06/2022): https://www.tinnitus.org.uk/

Brown, R.M. (1983) *Sudden Death.* Bantam: NYC.

Coalition for Collaborative Care/ NHS England, (2015, accessed 10/06/2022). *Personalised Care and Support Planning.* https://www.england.nhs.uk/ourwork/patient-participation/patient-centred/c4cc/

Dalal, F. (2019) *CBT: The Cognitive Behavioural Tsunami: Managerialism, Politics, and the Corruptions of Science.* Abingdon: Routledge

de Shazer, S. (1994) *Words Were Originally Magic.* NY: Norton.

Hoyt, M. (1996) *A Golfer's Guide to Brief Therapy in Constructive Therapies 2.* Guildford Press.

Improving Access to Psychological Therapies (UK-based, accessed 10/06/2022) https://www.england.nhs.uk/mental-health/adults/iapt/

Jackson, C. & Rizq, R. (2019) *The Industrialisation of Care: counselling, psychotherapy and the impact of IAPT.* Monmouth: PCCS Books.

NHS England. (2019, accessed 10/06/2022) *Personalised care factsheets* https://www.england.nhs.uk/publication/personalised-care-factsheets/

NICE (2004, accessed 10/06/2022) *Improving Supportive and Palliative Care for Adults with Cancer* https://www.nice.org.uk/guidance/csg4.

Royal Pharmaceutical Society of Great Britain (1997). *From compliance to concordance: Towards shared goals in medicine taking.* London: Royal Pharmaceutical Society of Great Britain.

Chapter 7

Barr, D. A. (2004). *Time to listen.* Annals of Internal Medicine, 41-44.

McCullagh, M. & Wright, R. (2008). *Good practice: communication skills in English for the medical practitioner.* Cambridge: Cambridge University Press.

Youngson, R. (2012). Time to care.: How to love your patients and your job. Raglan, New Zealand: Rebelheart Publishers.

Chapter 8

NICE (2009, UK-based, accessed 10/06/2022) *Medicines adherence: involving patients in decisions about prescribed medicines and supporting adherence.*
https://www.nice.org.uk/guidance/cg76/chapter/Introduction

Trueman, P. et al. (2010, accessed 10/06/2022) *Evaluation of the scale, causes and costs of waste medicines. Report of DH funded national project.* https://discovery.ucl.ac.uk/id/eprint/1350234/

Chapter 9

Brief: The Centre for Solution Focused Practice. (accessed 10/06/2022). https://www.brief.org.uk/

Lonsdale, P. (series from 1972 – 1992) *Rainbow.* ITV Studios.

ABOUT THE AUTHOR

Dr Dominic Bray (for some reason not looking at the camera)

Biography: Dominic Bray, M.A. (hons), Clin. Psy. D., C. Sci., A.F.B.P.S., C. Psychol. and Cycling Proficiency (failed) is an NHS consultant clinical psychologist in Sunny Southport who is very interested in developing healthcare conversations that help people with cancer and long-term conditions live what they would see as fulfilling and purposeful lives. These conversations may be his own in the form of psychological therapy, but, just as often, he spends time helping other health professionals to develop these skills. The backbone of his work is the solution-focused model, which construes people as co-experts with professionals in their own improvement towards living lives informed by what matters to them. Aside from all that, he has a family and a badly behaved Bichon dog, and drives a very dull car.